INTEGRATED CURRICULUM

SUSAN DRAKE

A Chapter of the
CURRICULUM
HANDBOOK

ASSOCIATION FOR SUPERVISION AND CURRICULUM DEVELOPMENT
ALEXANDRIA, VIRGINIA USA

Association for Supervision and Curriculum Development
1703 N. Beauregard St.   Alexandria, VA 22311-1714 USA
Telephone: 800-933-2723 or 703-578-9600   Fax: 703-575-5400
Web site: http://www.ascd.org   E-mail: member@ascd.org

Gene R. Carter
Executive Director

Scott Willis
Contributing Editor, ASCD Curriculum Handbook

Michelle Terry
Deputy Executive Director, Program Development

Terrey Hatcher Quindlen
Manager, Editorial Services

Nancy Modrak
Director, Publishing

Gary Bloom
Director, Design and Production Services

John Franklin
Managing Editor, ASCD Curriculum Handbook

Dina Murray Seamon
Production Coordinator

John O'Neil
Acquisitions Editor, ASCD Curriculum Handbook

Valerie Sprague
Desktop Publisher

Stock # 100004

ASCD Curriculum Handbook Distribution Policy

We encourage subscribers to the ASCD *Curriculum Handbook* to take full advantage of the contents of the *Curriculum Handbook*, within these guidelines:

• The subscriber has permission to make paper copies of materials in the ASCD *Curriculum Handbook* for fair use, such as staff development or curriculum committee meetings, provided that duplication is for an educational purpose in a not-for-profit institution, the resulting copies are made available without charge beyond the cost of reproduction, and each copy contains a full citation of the source.

• The permission to copy does not extend to copying the complete *Curriculum Handbook*, or any complete chapter. Permission does not transfer to those persons given reproduced materials by the subscriber.

• If the subscriber is an institution, this permission applies only to a single individual designated by the institution as the "subscriber."

• The *Curriculum Handbook* Web site contains all of the material included in the print version of the *Curriculum Handbook*, as well as additional material available only online. We encourage you to print paper copies of the Web site material (in accordance with the guidelines above), but we do not allow copying or distribution of the contents in an electronic form. If you have questions about the *Curriculum Handbook* distribution policy, please contact us at handbook@ascd.org.

• ASCD publications present a variety of viewpoints. The views expressed or implied in this book should not be interpreted as official positions of the Association.

Printed in the United States of America.

INTEGRATED CURRICULUM

ACKNOWLEDGMENTS

This piece could not have been written without the exciting experiences that so many educators shared with me. To these educators, I thank you very much for your generosity of both spirit and time. I also congratulate you on the innovative things you are doing in your classrooms and your courage for charting new territory.

I would like to acknowledge John O'Neil and John Franklin of ASCD for their thoughtful guidance on the route to publication.

Finally, I would like to thank a long list of reviewers who took the time to offer substantive feedback. This document is much richer for the insights of the following people.

Debra Attenborough, Art Director, Rodman Hall, St. Catharines, Ontario

Rebecca Burns, Curriculum Specialist, Appalachia Educational Laboratories, Charleston, West Virginia

Mae Denby, Retired Supervisory Officer, Artworld, St. Catharines, Ontario

Rosemary Hunter, Curriculum Specialist, Brock University, St. Catharines, Ontario

Tony Giblin, Math Instructor, Brock University, St. Catharines, Ontario

Mike McDonald, Consultant, Grand Erie District School Board, Ontario

Deborah Mindorff, Adult Educator, Brock University, St. Catharines, Ontario

Bob Ogilvie, Consultant, Grand Erie District School Board, Ontario

Len Popp, Curriculum Specialist, Brock University, St. Catharines, Ontario

Janie Senko, Teacher, Grand Erie District School Board, Ontario

Jack Whitehead, Professor, University of Bath, Bath, Great Britain

I. OVERVIEW

I was counting the days until I retired. But now I'm doing all this interesting integration stuff and I've decided to stay on.

        —Rob McDowell, high school teacher

Integrated curriculum. It's what I do. It's my PASSION!!

        —Janie Senko, grade 5 teacher

I told the students it was a special project because I wanted them to be serious and stay with it—"It will require you to go out and take a chance and meet interesting people, professional people"—and they really, really loved it.

        —Grade 11 teacher in the Millennium Project

Teachers involved in integrated curriculum projects are excited about what is going on in their classrooms. Clearly something is happening that is not necessarily happening in every classroom. This document has been written primarily as a resource guide for those in curriculum administration; however, it will also be relevant to teachers. It provides an overview of integrated curriculum and a practical guide to implementing integrated curriculum in the classroom. The intent of this document is to offer an interdisciplinary approach to integrated curriculum that is standards-based and meaningful to both teachers and students.

Curriculum integration is a complex topic because every aspect of education is involved. It is not simply putting together content from different subject areas. If one is contemplating interdisciplinary approaches, many of the fundamental questions of education must be considered. This chapter begins to explore these questions.

The first section will address questions such as what is integrated curriculum and why it should be used. This consideration will include a brief look at the history of integrated curriculum and research on integrated curriculum in education.

The second section examines current directions in education, primarily within Ontario and the United States, and provides examples of current tensions and emerging patterns. The accountability issues of standards, assessment, and evaluation are discussed within the context of integrated curriculum. What knowledge and skills are worth knowing and doing as this new century unfolds is also considered in this light. The remainder of this section addresses new views of how we learn and the implications of new ways to understand learning and knowing, in relation to how we should teach and assess students.

The third section illustrates two models for planning an interdisciplinary curriculum. Both a standards-based model and a problem-based model are provided, along with recommendations for implementation and a sample of applying the models in practice. This section also describes seven examples of integrated curriculum that are being implemented successfully in classrooms today. These include both primary and secondary school examples, ranging from one or a few teachers to 60, and from integrating a few disciplines to a fully integrated program. This section provides a practical illustration of the scope of application and complexity that integrated curriculum can address.

The fourth section provides a list of commonly asked questions and the answers. These questions are relevant to both administrators and teachers because they address issues of concern from both an institutional and individual level and offer many tested and practical suggestions.

The next two sections list other resources available on integrated curriculum.

WHY INTEGRATE THE CURRICULUM?

We are living in a complex age, and life has never been segmented into disciplines. Living is experienced as an integrated whole. To live successfully, one needs skills that cut across the disciplines. For example, consider the skills and knowledge necessary for so seemingly simple an act as grocery shopping for a nutritious, balanced, and economical diet. Before one even begins to shop, there are some essential things the shopper must know and be able to do. How do you know the difference between nutritional and junk foods? The ability to read and understand labels on food products is crucial to making nutritional choices. To select the correct amount of each product, the number of people to be served and the recommended proportions of the four food groups need to be considered. In order to buy economically, one must be able to calculate the difference in prices between seemingly similar products. Finally, one needs interpersonal skills to be able to ask for help from grocery personnel when it is needed.

Today, fundamental change is occurring in every aspect of life. Technological advances have thrust us into a global world where many of our tried and true assumptions are being challenged. The very definitions of such fundamentals as family, health care, and economy are shifting. The cutting-edge jobs are going to people who can think outside of traditional "boxes." Employers increasingly are looking to hire generalists with "soft skills" such as leadership and change management. They want sophisticated problem solvers who can think critically and thus deal with ill-structured, complex problems. They want self-directed people who are willing and able to continually learn new things. In many cases, the technological skills needed in a job are changing so rapidly that schools can't keep up. Employers also are finding that it is the soft skills that make the difference between a successful and unsuccessful employee.

Education is also changing fundamentally. What is worth knowing? How can we make curriculum relevant? How do schools produce the type of productive citizens needed in this new century? How can students be encouraged to become self-directed, critical, and creative thinkers who excel at problem solving? How can we move toward making "success for all" a reality?

To address these questions many educators are turning toward curriculum that is situated in a real-life context. This type of curriculum tends to be student-centered and experiential and revolve around problem solving, making many of these efforts interdisciplinary by nature.

Integrated curriculum is an approach that can address many current issues. It can, for example,

■ Reduce duplication of skills and concepts in different subject areas.
■ Increase relevance for the learner, given a real-life context.
■ Allow for the learner to see the big picture, rather than just the fragmented parts.
■ Allow for teaching interdisciplinary life skills for the 21st century.
■ Focus on skills that can be transferred to other disciplines and to life.

Integration by itself, however, is no panacea. A curriculum can be totally integrated in its content and still leave the learners disinterested if it is delivered in a lifeless manner. What makes a difference in an integrated approach is not only what is taught but *how* it is taught. Integrated curriculum is usually delivered with strategies such as active learning, experiential learning, problem solving, and real-life contexts.

WHAT IS INTEGRATED CURRICULUM?

One of the problems with integrated curriculum is that it can mean many things to different people.

Integrated curriculum is about making meaningful connections between topics or skills that are usually addressed in different subject areas. However, over time there have been many different definitions, describing approaches that varied philosophically. To complicate things further, integrated approaches can range from a small unit of study in one classroom to a fully integrated day in an entire school.

Many theorists argue that levels of integration can be found on a continuum (see, for example, Burns, 1995; Drake, 1998; Fogarty, 1991; Jacobs, 1989). At the lowest level, teachers have begun to integrate the curriculum in several ways.

Fusion, for example, is when a specific theme or skill is fused into separate subject areas. Technology across the curriculum is often dealt with in this way. Another example of a lower level of integration is when various subdisciplines are integrated. Integrating biology, chemistry, and physics, for example, is now common even at the university level.

In Ontario, grades 1 to 9 were officially required to use an integrated, outcome-based approach in *The Common Curriculum* (1993, 1995). During those years, I observed many educators planning for integrated approaches and was personally involved in several ventures. Based on these experiences, I developed a continuum of three approaches that I saw people adopting (Drake, 1993). The three approaches were multidisciplinary, interdisciplinary, and transdisciplinary. They are represented in three integrated curriculum models that show each model's approach and conceptual framework (see Figure 1.1). A brief description of each model is provided below.

Multidisciplinary

In a multidisciplinary approach, two or more subject areas are organized around the same theme or topic. In elementary school, this often occurs when learning centers are utilized. The topic may be pioneers, and students rotate through a math center, language center, and visual art center. At each one they explore the topic of pioneers via an activity grounded in the curriculum subject area.

In secondary schools, a common theme is often studied in various subject-based classrooms. For example, teachers of all subject areas at Skyview High School in Smithfield, Utah, and North Cache 8–9 Center in Richmond, Utah, have agreed to integrate the public health issue of physical activity into their lesson plans (Eckman, 2000). They undertook this integration in concert with the Utah Department of Health. Social studies was to look at policymaking procedures, and English was to write editorials and public service announcements about the issue. In math class students learned graphing, plotting, percentages, and ratios as they pertain to collecting health data. Sociology and psychology students were to implement and test planned intervention.

Another popular multidisciplinary approach is to view the content through a number of disciplinary lenses. This usually involves a problem or an issue. Students systematically ask, for example, how a scientist, an artist, or a mathematician would approach this problem.

There is an attempt at making explicit connections across subject areas. This often happens in a culminating activity. For example, in an integrated arts unit, students have studied visual arts, drama, and music separately but have connected the skills they learned in a final musical performance (Sturch, 1996).

Interdisciplinary

In this approach, interdisciplinary skills are the organizing center for two or more subject areas. These are process skills such as research, literacy, or numeracy skills. Connections are also made with content through the teaching of concepts that cut across subject areas.

FIGURE 1.1
Three Integrated Curriculum Models

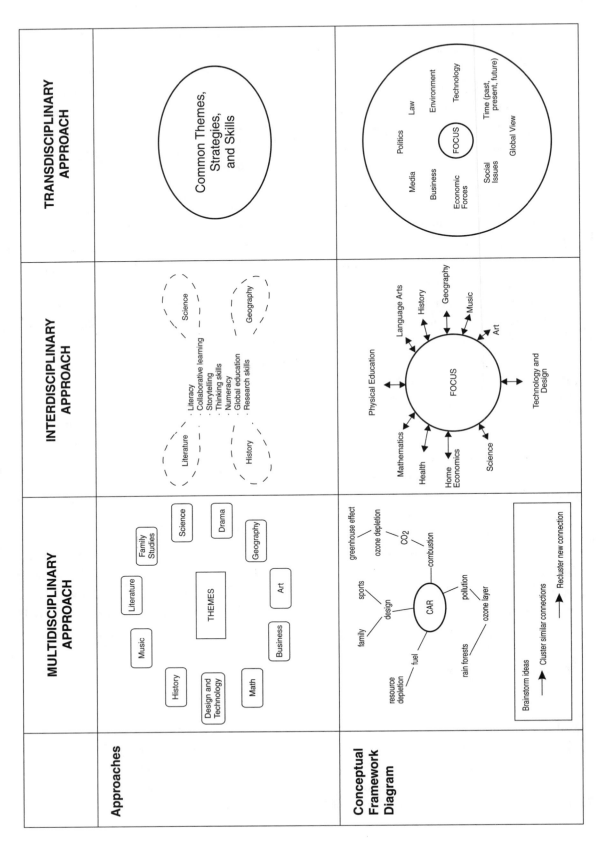

A good example of this is in a schoolwide grade 7–8 unit, four to six weeks long, developed by teachers from Peter Muhlenburg Middle School, Woodstock, Va. (Burns, 1995). The focus of study was "survival in a changing world." All subject areas were involved in the unit, including a foreign language, agriculture, and life management. All teachers focused on problem solving, decision making, and communication, and selected the concepts that were most compatible with their course content.

This approach lends itself very well to planning with standards and performance assessment because the standards for each discipline are clearly set out. They can be "reclustered" into interdisciplinary clusters that fit together naturally. The culminating activity is also usually performance-based and is grounded in the standards taught throughout the unit.

Transdisciplinary

In the transdisciplinary approach there is a real-life context, and student needs act as the organizing center. The disciplines are not considered in the initial planning stages. The assumption is that most or all disciplines are embedded in the topic of study and can be isolated if so desired.

The Kids Around Town (KAT) Project, a pilot local-government education program in Pennsylvania, is a good example of a curriculum organized around a real-life context (Rappoport & Kletzien, 1996). Fifth-graders select a public policy issue that affects them locally. The issue, such as litter in a local park, is the catalyst for study and analysis, planning strategies, and actions. The goal is for students to understand the process of formulating public policy. There is no textbook; the program emphasizes multiple information sources and multiple solutions.

Project-based learning often fits this category. Such an approach was used, for example, by Dot Schuler, who teaches 2nd grade at Grafton Elementary School, Grafton, Ill. (Fleming, in press). Her students studied water for six weeks. To begin, the students brainstormed for ideas to create a web. As the ideas were shared, the students and Dot decided on a name for a category to group the ideas in. For example, when children shared the words "shark, bass, catfish," they would decide to call the category "things that live in water." If the students named "pipes, buckets, puddles," the category might be called "places to find water." Personal stories were recorded and placed in the listening center, along with a movie box portraying each child's illustrations for his or her story. Schuler posed open-ended questions, and the children published the responses on charts as a reference for the rest of the project.

Students were exposed to numerous real-life "water" contexts in the community, such as the local water park and the Grafton Water Works. Investigations were created from the students' questions. Two class books focusing on alliteration and descriptive essays were written featuring descriptions from students' personal experiences and knowledge. Three class math books were made featuring two-step story problems, number words, and fractions. The application of curricular skills abounded; some occurred naturally, others were taught systematically. Other examples of project-based learning can be found at Schuler's Web site, http://www.plantnet.com/dschuler/.

The work of Beane (1993) is another wonderful example of transdisciplinary curriculum because it draws on the needs and concerns of the student. He begins the curriculum planning with two fundamental questions:

1. What questions and concerns do you have about yourself?
2. What questions and concerns do you have about your world?

The themes of study emerge from the answers students give to these questions. Although Beane begins with the students' interests and needs, he does not abandon the disciplines. For him, disciplines are used as resources to explore the theme and to create teaching and learning activities. The Alpha Program in Section III offers a detailed example of this approach.

Figure 1.1 offers a framework through which to reflect on the concept of a continuum. Although this framework was developed in 1993, for the most part it still holds true. As we gain more experience with integration, however, the boundaries between subjects become more and more blurred. A pitfall to using a continuum is that it can be value-laden (Hargreaves et al., 1996). In reality, one approach is not superior to another. However, one may be more appropriate than another in certain circumstances.

Pursuing the Interdisciplinary Approach

Multidisciplinary curriculum is perhaps the easiest way to begin integrating the curriculum. For many teachers, transdisciplinary curriculum is experienced as the most natural way to develop meaningful and relevant curriculum. Yet we are living in an age of accountability, when the standards movement and a focused interest in assessment are not likely to go away quickly or quietly. For this reason, the interdisciplinary approach appears to fit best with current realities. However, it is the most challenging approach for teachers to develop and deliver, as it goes against the grain of long-held practices. Over time some teachers have demonstrated that they can plan with standards in ways that result in relevant and meaningful interdisciplinary curriculum.

This *Curriculum Handbook* chapter will focus on the interdisciplinary approach. Powell (1999) asserts that interdisciplinary approaches might still be delivered in a traditional format whereby the teacher lectures and the students passively receive

knowledge. Integrative approaches, on the other hand, promote an active learning model in which students construct knowledge in a democratic classroom.

In this chapter, however, all integrated curriculum delivery is assumed to be student-centered in classrooms that feature active integrative learning. The words interdisciplinary and integrated will be used interchangeably. Similarly, I define the term "standards" broadly to include such ideas as competencies, expectations, and outcomes. Standards, in my definition, include both content standards and performance standards. The intent of this chapter is to provide a way to plan curriculum that satisfies current demands for the attainment of standards and also offers benefits of an integrated curriculum.

RESEARCH IN EDUCATION

In the last decade, a lot has been written on integrated curriculum. Articles tend to discuss the theory and merits of integration, describe the process, or provide case studies. Czerniak and colleagues (1999), for example, review the literature on integrated curriculum and offer an excellent look at the state of the art. They discuss several issues: the lack of an operational definition of integrated curriculum, the role of integration in school curriculum, advantages and disadvantages, and problems associated with implementation. The authors also lament the lack of empirical studies in the field.

A dialogue on interdisciplinary curriculum theory has continued over the past few years. Integrated curriculum has been attacked as not rigorous enough (Case, 1994). Rigor can be created when three criteria are present: substance, relevance, and coherence (Martin-Kniep, Feige, & Soodak, 1995). The content needs to be significant, and teachers need to be grounded in their subject fields. A relevant curriculum is one that is interpreted by practicing teachers as skill-building for future careers and providing awareness of students' social and political contexts (Hargreaves & Moore, 2000). Hargreaves and Moore note that integrated curriculum, rather than being superficial, can be rigorous and demanding of both the students and teacher.

HISTORY OF INTEGRATED CURRICULUM

It is useful to know that interdisciplinary curriculum is not just a fad. For more than a century, there have been a number of forays into the realm of integrated curriculum. The following brief historical account is based on the excellent work of Wraga (1996, 1997) found in the *Annual Review of Research for School Leaders*.

By the late 1800s, educators were wrestling with many of the same concerns we now face more than a century later. Three pressing issues gave rise to discussions on the pros and cons of integrated curriculum and instruction:

1. What should be taught, given the vast increase in available knowledge?
2. What should be taught, given the greater number of students who now need to be educated?
3. How can schools be responsible for developing moral character unless the curriculum is connected to real life?

In the late 1800s, these discussions were at the theory level only. Resistance to integrated approaches was attributed to similar reasons as are touted today. They included:

■ Varying definitions for varying degrees of integration, ranging from simple connections between subjects to integrating students' experience with the larger world.
■ The importance of making the school experience applicable to life.

■ The domination of the disciplines as an obstacle to integration.

In 1900, John Dewey proposed: "Relate the school to life, and all studies are of necessity correlated" (Dewey, 1900, p. 91). Dewey experimented with an experiential approach, proposing experiences of growth for students. Problem solving through the scientific method was at the core of this process. His philosophy has been largely associated with the progressive education movement; however, Dewey did not agree with all the movement's tenets, arguing for more rigor through the scientific method.

By the 1930s, three progressive approaches emerged: the project method, the experience curriculum, and the activity movement. These approaches, however, tended to be extremely child-centered and emphasized activity for activity's sake. Curriculum organizations emerged to bring more rigor to progressive approaches. Statewide curriculum development projects were undertaken in Virginia, Arkansas, Kentucky, Texas, Georgia, and Tennessee. It was determined that 80 percent of schools in the United States had some form of interdisciplinary curriculum

At the same time, general education advocates promoted "common learning." Such experiences included problem solving, critical thinking, and analytical research. "Core curriculum" emerged from general education. In core curriculum, learning activities and knowledge were organized around personal and social issues. It involved block timing and team teaching. Core curriculum remained popular during the 1940s and '50s. In 1955, ASCD issued a report identifying the following competencies for a core teacher using an interdisciplinary approach: understanding the adolescent, democratic leadership skills, student counseling skills, and the ability to apply subject knowledge to exploring personal and social issues.

Integrated curriculum approaches were largely

forgotten during the Sputnik crisis in the late '50s. At this time, the educational world was plunged into a rigid, discipline-based approach with a special emphasis on math and sciences. Two innovations, however, left the door open for discussions on integrated approaches: team teaching and the emergence of middle schools.

By the late 1980s there were new calls for reform in papers such as *Caught in the Middle* (California State Department of Education, 1987) and *Turning Points* (Carnegie Council on Adolescent Development, 1989). These papers focused on making school relevant for students. Attention turned again to integrated curriculum.

Seeking Academic Success

Case studies tend to tell the same story: Students do well in integrated studies; they are engaged in the study; and they learn skills beyond the set curriculum. Unfortunately, this does not convince those who want to have "hard data" that curriculum integration works before they will venture forward. There is, however, encouraging research to support curriculum integration efforts. Some of this research is presented here.

The Eight-Year Study, done in the 1930s, offers the most dramatic example of what can happen in high schools if integrated curriculum is taught (Aikin, 1942). Thirty secondary schools and 1,475 students participated in this study. Researchers investigated how well students would do in higher education if they were educated in schools that were student-centered and learned the skills and social orientation for a democratic way of life.

In the study, schools were given the freedom to decide how they would present curriculum to students. Colleges and universities dropped admission requirements, subject and credit prescriptions, and, in most cases, entrance exams. This facilitated the high schools' adoption of innovative programs to deliver the curriculum. Matched pairs of students (in the study and from a traditional school not in the study) were compared on 18 variables including academic honors, grade average, objective thinking, cocurricular activities and community involvement. The graduates of the 30 schools did "somewhat better" than the comparison group (Aikin, 1942, p. 112). The graduates from the most experimental schools, where interdisciplinary work was an important characteristic, were "strikingly more successful" (p. 113) than their matches in all other schools in the study. On the other hand, the graduates from the least innovative schools showed no differences from the comparison group.

This study has had little influence in the educational community — perhaps because the project ended just at the beginning of World War II. It is unfortunate, since there was never again such large-scale research. Quantitative studies of integration projects are hard to come by. For some, this is because confusion surrounds what qualifies as an interdisciplinary program. For others, quantitative approaches do not fit what they are trying to measure.

Given the current domination of standardized tests, people want to know the relationship between integrated approaches and success on such tests. Unfortunately, there is still little evidence on how students fare on standardized tests. As districts move into more systematic interdisciplinary programs, however, data are becoming available. The following are some examples:

1. Burns (1994) reports that Interdisciplinary Teamed Instruction had positive effects on student performance, particularly for lower-achieving students in four sites. By 1998, three of these sites, which used interdisciplinary instruction for more than two years, reported an overall upward trend in standardized test scores (Burns, in press).

2. Caine and Caine (1997) also report an upward

trend in standardized test scores in two case studies of elementary schools.

3. Twenty-eight of the 100 middle schools that were examined as effective reported specific results demonstrating improved scores on standardized tests (George & Oldaker, 1985).

4. Students enrolled in a three-year integrated science program performed 4 percentiles higher, which is marginally significant, than 121 matched students not in the program (University of Alabama Center for Communication and Educational Technology, 1997).

5. Lieberman and Hoody (1998) offer solid evidence that integrated environmental programs work. A significant improvement in student performance in reading, writing, math, science, and social studies was documented across 40 American schools.

6. More than 100 3rd grade students who took an integrated science and literature course did significantly better on all literacy measures than children in a literature-only group. Children in the literature-only group did significantly better than the children in the control group (traditional classroom), except on standardized reading tests. The literature and science group did significantly better than either of the other two groups on science concepts (Guthrie et al., 1998).

7. At Radnor Middle School in Pennsylvania, about one-fifth of the grade 7 students study the watershed all year in a fully integrated program. Over the nine years of the program, these students have shown consistently the greatest writing improvement, compared with the students in the traditional classroom. Their standardized test scores are equal to or better than the other students' (Sadowski, 1995).

8. Green (1991) reports increased student interest and achievement scores on the NAEP (National Assessment of Educational Progress) for students in California who participated in thematic units.

9. A powerful example of the potential of interdisciplinary curriculum is International High School, New York (Sadowski, 1995), Here, interdisciplinary curriculum is taught all day. The school has a graduation rate of over 95 percent, and over 90 percent of graduates go on to college. Virtually all students pass the New York Regency Competency tests in all subjects. This is extraordinary when you consider that the 450 students have been in the United States for less than four years and have low English proficiency scores.

Other Benefits to Students

Vars (1996) reviewed more than 100 programs that took place between 1956 and 1995. At that time, he concluded that integrative approaches are beneficial to students in many ways. Beane (1995) also echoed this conclusion. Vars (2000a) restated the accuracy of his 1996 claim:

> Almost without exception, students in innovative interdisciplinary programs do as well as, and often better than, students in so-called conventional programs. In other words, educators who carefully implement any of the various types of interdisciplinary approaches can be reasonably assured that there will be no appreciable loss in student learning— except, perhaps, for the temporary "implementation dip" that occurs whenever people try anything new. (1996, p. 149).

Although there may not be much data yet on links between interdisciplinary education and standardized tests, there is abundant evidence of other benefits. Much of this evidence is anecdotal, but the evidence mounts. An overview of these benefits can be found in *Creating Integrated Curriculum: Proven Ways to Increase Student Learning* (Drake, 1998).

Studies cited in this book claim that interdisciplinary work

■ Increased learning.
■ Led to greater personal growth.
■ Boosted self-motivation.
■ Increased the ability to apply concepts.
■ Led to better understanding of science concepts.
■ Increased student motivation.
■ Led students to become more responsible human beings.
■ Fostered better writing skills.
■ Increased positive attitudes toward reading.
■ Enhanced self-confidence.
■ Increased student cooperation.
■ Reduced disruptive behavior.
■ Reduced math anxiety.
■ Increased use of higher thinking skills.
■ Improved the quality of work.

Given these potential results including academic success, it is little wonder that teachers who use interdisciplinary methods are convinced that they are an effective, if not better, way to learn.

The Process of Integration

Much of the literature revolves around the process of integration. Rebecca Burn's *Dissolving the Boundaries* (1995) is an excellent research-based resource. She discusses various definitions of integration, assessing the readiness of the school culture, and preparing teams for integration. This is a good resource for anyone who wants to facilitate the process of curriculum integration, as it offers a step-by-step process for preparing people to plan for curriculum. The process of integration, along with current research and applications of several models of integration, are offered in *Creating Integrated Curriculum: Proven Ways to Increase Student Learning* (Drake, 1998).

Two factors are often discussed as integral to integrated curriculum: teaming and block scheduling. Teaming has many advantages. According to data from 155 middle schools, common planning time was crucial to success (Flowers, Mertens, & Mulhall, 1999). Those involved believed that teaming

■ Improved school climate.
■ Improved work climate.
■ Increased parental contact.
■ Increased job satisfaction.

Block scheduling has also been touted as necessary to integrate curriculum properly and is a central component of core curriculum. Certainly, schools that integrate usually do change the schedule to allow for more time in the classroom. Vars (1996) offers the following advantages to block scheduling:

■ Teachers have fewer pupils for longer periods.
■ Pupils have fewer teachers.
■ The same teacher teaches one group of students two or more subject areas.

These advantages lead to better opportunities for creative teaching and learning activities, time to provide for individual differences, greater security for the student, and more opportunity for teacher-student planning and cooperative evaluation.

Vars (2000b) also offers the experiences of Betty Bickford, a teacher from Lincoln, Maine. She found she can integrate within a 40-minute classroom period. She followed Beane's model (1993) and began with student questions. They worked on the theme of relationships and demonstrated the results of their research in a PowerPoint presentation given in a game format. Students developed assessment rubrics and assessed how well the unit aligned with district curriculum and Maine's Learning Results.

In summary, the research supports integrated approaches. Students do at least as well, or better, on standardized tests than students in regular programs. The added benefits make teaching and learning a more exciting and engaging enterprise. As we enter an era of data-driven decision making, we can expect that more empirical studies will be added to the knowledge base.

WORKS CITED

Aikin, W. M. (1942). *The story of the eight-year study.* New York: Harper.

Beane, J. (1993). *A middle school curriculum: From rhetoric to reality.* Columbus, OH: National Middle School Association.

Beane, J. (1995). Curriculum integration and the disciplines of knowledge. *Phi Delta Kappan, 76* (8), 616–622.

Burns, R. C. (1994). *Interdisciplinary teamed instruction: Development and pilot test.* Charleston, WV: Appalachia Educational Laboratory. (ED 384–456)

Burns, R. C. (1995). *Dissolving the boundaries: Planning for curriculum integration in middle and secondary schools.* Charleston, WV: Appalachia Educational Laboratory.

Burns, R. C. (in press). Interdisciplinary teamed instruction. In J. T. Klein (Ed.), *Integrated and interdisciplinary curriculum across K–16.* New York: The College Board.

Caine, R., & Caine, G. (1997). *Education on the edge of possibility.* Alexandria, VA: Association for Supervision and Curriculum Development.

California State Department of Education. (1987). *Caught in the middle.* Sacramento, CA: Author.

Carnegie Council on Adolescent Development. (1989). *Turning points: Preparing American youth for the 21st century.* Washington, DC: Carnegie Corporation.

Case, R. (1994). Our crude handling of curriculum reform: The case of curriculum integration. *Canadian Journal of Education, 19*(1), 80–93.

Czerniak, C. M., Weber, W. B., Sandmann, A., & Adhern, J. (1999). A literature review of science and mathematics integration. *School Science and Mathematics, 99*(8), 421–430.

Dewey J. (1956/1902/1900). *The child and the curriculum/The school and society.* Chicago: University of Chicago Press.

Drake, S. M. (1993). *Planning integrated curriculum: The call to adventure.* Alexandria, VA: Association for Supervision and Curriculum Development.

Drake, S. M. (1998). *Creating integrated curriculum: Proven ways to increase student learning.* Thousand Oaks, CA: Corwin.

Eckman, A. (2000, Spring). Tackling real world issues. *Curriculum Update,* 4–5.

Fogarty, R. (1991). *The mindful school: How to integrate the curricula.* Palatine, IL: SkyLight.

Fleming, D. S. (in press). *A teacher's guide to project-based learning.* Charleston, WV: Appalachia Educational Laboratory.

Flowers, N., Mertens, S. B., & Mulhall, P. F. (1999). The impact of teaming: Five research-based outcomes. *Middle School Journal, 31*(2), 57–60.

George, P. S., & Oldaker, L. L. (1985). *Evidence for the middle school.* Columbus, OH: National Middle School Association.

Greene, L. C. (1991, October). Science-centered curriculum in elementary school. *Educational Leadership, 49*(2), 42–51.

Guthrie, J. T., Van Meta, P., Hancock, G. R., Alao, S., Anderson, E., & McCann, A. A. (1998). Does concept-oriented reading instruction increase strategy use and conceptual learning from text? *Journal of Educational Psychology, 90*(2), 261–278.

Hargreaves, A., & Moore, S. (2000). Curriculum integration and classroom relevance: A study of teachers' practice. *Journal of Curriculum and Supervision, 15*(2), 89–112.

Hargreaves. A., Earl, L., & Ryan, J. (1996). *Schooling for change: Reinventing education for early adolescents.* London: Falmer Press.

Jacobs, H. H. (Ed.). (1989). *Interdisciplinary curriculum: Design and development.* Alexandria, VA: Association for Supervision and Curriculum Development.

Lieberman, G. A., & Hoody, L. L. (1998). *Closing the achievement gap: Using the environment as an integrating context for learning.* San Diego, CA: State Education and Environment Roundtable.

Martin-Kniep, G. O., Feige, D. M., & Soodak, L. C. (1995). Curriculum integration: An expanded view of an abused idea. *Journal of Supervision and Curriculum, 10*(3), 227–249.

Ontario Ministry of Education (1993, 1995). *The common curriculum: policies and outcomes, grades 1–9.* Toronto: Ministry of Education and Training, Government of Ontario.

Powell, R. R. (1999). Reflections on integrative curriculum: A conversation with Camille Barr and Molly Maloy. *Middle School Journal, 31*(2), 25–34.

Rappoport, A. L., & Kletzien, S. (1996, May). Kids around town: Civic lessons leave impressions. *Educational Leadership, 53*(8), 26–29.

Sadowski, M. (1995). Moving beyond traditional subjects requires teachers to abandon their "comfort zones." *The Harvard Education Letter, 11*(2), 1–6.

Sturch, J. E. (1996). The arts quest: Integrating drama, music and visual arts. *Orbit, 27*(1), 36–37.

University of Alabama Center for Communication and Educational Technology. (1997). *Summary report of the Integrated Science Student Impact Study.* Birmingham, AL: Author.

Vars, G. F. (1996). Effects of interdisciplinary curriculum and instruction. In P. Hlebowitch & W. Wraga (Eds.), *Annual review of research for school leaders* (pp. 148–164). New York: Scholastic.

Vars, G. F. (2000a). Editorial comment: On research, high-stakes testing, and core philosophy. *The Core Teacher, 50*(3), 1.

Vars, G. F. (2000b). "Relationships" unit makes English classes more integrative and democratic. *The Core Teacher, 51*, 3.

Wraga, W. (1996). A century of interdisciplinary curricula in American schools. In P. Hlebowitch & W. Wraga (Eds.), *Annual review of research for school leaders* (pp. 118–145). New York: Scholastic.

Wraga, W. (1997). Patterns of interdisciplinary curriculum organization and professional knowledge of the curriculum field. *Journal of Curriculum and Supervision, 12*(2), 98–117.

II. MAJOR TRENDS AND ISSUES

CURRENT DIRECTIONS IN EDUCATION

In the midst of dramatically changing times, there is a constant call for educational reform. Educators find themselves in a context of great tension. The concept of what is worth knowing is shifting. Competency in reading, writing, and arithmetic (the three Rs) is no longer enough. To be prepared for a highly technological world, students need to be technologically literate. They need process skills, such as information management, and higher-order thinking abilities, such as critical thinking, to make sense of the Internet. Communication skills are essential for the workplace. These enriched additional abilities are often referred to as the "new basics." They include, but go far beyond, the traditional notion of the three Rs.

There are also new understandings of how people learn. This has led to a renewed search for effective teaching and assessment strategies to ensure that *all* students learn optimally. Integration has come to be associated with both of these interests. Interdisciplinary curriculum tends to focus both on the new basics and on innovative teaching and assessment strategies.

In seeming contrast, there is a simultaneous move toward accountability that involves standards and evaluation through standardized testing. Innovative ways of teaching are often attacked as the culprit in a "weaker" educational system and the reason why such accountability measures are necessary. Yet, as Kohn points out (O'Neil & Tell, 1999), innovative pedagogy is hardly the norm in our schools; thus it appears more likely that it is the traditional models that are failing our students. Similarly, integration by itself is no panacea. It can be just as deadly as any other curriculum—it depends on the delivery model. The challenge is to develop and implement effective teaching and assessment strategies that both satisfy accountability measures and are based on how people learn.

Current Tensions

Events in Ontario typify the tensions between different curriculum orientations. In 1990, Hargreaves and Earl's *Rights of Passage* catapulted schools into reform. Ontario's *The Common Curriculum* (1993, 1995) mandated an integrated, outcomes-based approach for grades 1 to 9. Just as teachers were beginning to appreciate this approach, a newly elected government replaced the 1995 curriculum with eight discipline-based support documents. These new documents included hundreds of explicit, discipline-based standards (expectations) to replace the more amorphous outcomes for grades 1 to 8 in *The Common Curriculum* (1993, 1995). A standardized provincial report card was issued and forced teachers to learn new technology. Provincial testing was introduced at grades 3, 6, and 9 in reading, writing, and mathematics. At the same time, there was a retrenchment from "official" integration.

The experience of Centennial Public School, under the Halton District School Board, is typical of what happened in schools that taught integrated curriculum in Ontario. Scott (1999) followed the teachers for seven years. It took them three years to become comfortable with integration. They declared that they could never return to a segmented form of curriculum delivery. Then they were hit with the government's new program and reduced resources. In particular, the new detailed, discipline-based report card was an obstacle to integration. Overwhelmed, the teachers began to back away from their attempts at integration. Today they are struggling to find ways to adapt to the new demands and still keep an integrated approach.

Emerging Patterns

Within this context of tension, a pattern is emerging. Some teachers are finding that they can indeed adopt interdisciplinary approaches and still honor the accountability movement. They claim interdisciplinary work is a more effective way to reach students. They are becoming familiar with the most recent discipline-based standards and are once again able to see the connections and the common learning across subject areas.

Janie Senko, a grade 5 teacher from Grand Erie District School Board, Ontario, offers the following description of an experience like this:

Right now I am doing an early civilization theme, as mandated by the social studies curriculum. I literally handed it over to my students to plan. I equipped them with excellent resources, and they came up with the learning activities. It's so exciting to see the natural integration and overlapping of subject areas.

Here is an example. The Grade 5 social studies curriculum says that I need to teach my students about early civilizations. To begin this, we did a novel study with a book called The Royal Diaries: Cleopatra VII, Daughter of the Nile, Egypt, 57 B.C. *(Gregory, 1999). Reading this novel, discussing it, and responding to it satisfied many of the following standards:*

■ *Social studies—food, shelter, clothing, cultural practices, nature of government, values and beliefs, architecture.*
■ *Health—food, values and beliefs.*
■ *Music—ancient instruments and cultural practices.*
■ *Drama and dance—we are creating a play and will act it out in class.*
■ *Language arts—communicating and summarizing information, writing using a variety of forms, reading and describing events, discussing plot, characters, making judgments, and so forth.*

It is really like the snowball effect. There are

about 400 or 500 standards to cover. Everything interconnects and amazingly you "knock off" a large number of standards across the curriculum with fewer activities.

The early civilization theme was introduced through the novel; it was historically accurate. I also saturated the room with a collection of books about a variety of early civilizations. As the theme developed, students learned a great deal about the Egyptian and Roman cultures from the novel alone. They acted out the story in a play format. The play alone incorporated a number of subject areas, social studies, language arts, and music. We had a great time creating papier-mâché, Egyptian canopic jars, Greek masks, or Roman head rests. Students were able to choose which one of these they wished to make. We constructed (through precise measurement) models of Roman aqueducts, Greek temples, and Roman homes. We had a sand table with the Nile River. We used sand as well as soil for this, as the banks of the Nile have soil. We sowed grass along the banks of the Nile. The grass grew tall. The desert remained grassless.

We designed rubrics together for the assessment of the research projects and the arts. There is teacher, peer, and self-assessment for these. Students keep response journals about all the subject areas: these are used for language assessment. Science labs are marked separately, and I give a math test. There is a quiz on the whole unit at the end.

My students were genuinely enthralled by this unit of study. It is their unit. They created it. I believe they learned so much. In fact, I took them to the Royal Ontario Museum in Toronto to see the Ancient Egyptian Art Exhibit. I was astounded to hear all that they knew as they responded to the questions of the tour guides. One of my students was able to list all of the specific organs that were put into the specific canopic jars. Another student explained how the organs were removed from the corpse. A third student explained why the male and female statues were colored differently.

Across North America there are similar issues with accountability, emphasizing a return to the basics, disciplines, and standardized testing. Much of the testing is high stakes, so teachers are forced to take it seriously and teach in ways that optimize students' chances at success. For many, this direction contradicts integrated approaches and is perceived as an almost insurmountable obstacle.

Yet almost every national reform effort is stressing the need to integrate. According to Czerniak and colleagues (1999), contemporary organizations such as the National Council of Teachers of English (NCTE), National Council for the Social Studies (NCSS), the National Council of Teachers of Mathematics (NCTM), and the National Science Teachers Association (NSTA) are recommending making connections across subject areas. Interestingly, countries such as Japan and Norway are mandating integrated approaches in parts of their curriculum (Vars, 2000). These two countries are perceived to have rigor and accountability in their curricula. If indeed the spirit of integration is in their delivery models, it seems that we can develop rigorous integrated curriculum that maintains accountability.

IN SEARCH OF ACCOUNTABILITY

It is possible to merge accountability with innovative teaching and assessing. I have had a wide range of experience with both researching and being directly involved in systemic change. The goal of the changes was a restructured system that valued constructivist approaches in the classroom. The official mandate included interdisciplinary work, alternative assessment, and standards. Some boards or districts chose to focus on implementing standards, including skills and content standards; others looked at a variety of assessment practices and evaluation;

still others focused on developing integrated curriculum. The new mandates were too unfamiliar for any board to try to incorporate all three aspects at once. Yet each of the paths connected with one of the others. The integrated curriculum district, for example, found that it had to address evaluation and that standards were an integral part both of integrating curriculum and of assessment. This happened with all the boards involved in restructuring, regardless of the starting point.

Standards

Standards can actually open the door to interdisciplinary work. First, we are learning to be more and more explicit about what we expect from students. This clarifies both the teachers' task and the students' understanding of what they need to know and do in order to demonstrate that they meet the standard. Second, standards are being developed all over the country and at all levels, from national to local. The number of common learning experiences across the subject areas is becoming increasingly evident. They transcend the disciplines and are skill based. They are the new basics.

Standards (expectations, competencies, and outcomes) emerged as a way of determining what students can know and do at the end of an educational experience or at key stages in their development. In the United States, professional organizations took the lead in developing standards for their disciplines. The National Council of Teachers of Mathematics, for example, was the first to issue standards for students, which it did in 1989. By 2000, all of the professional associations representing the school subjects had issued standards for what students should know and be able to do. In addition, nearly all states, and many districts, have created standards for students.

As a result, many teachers today need to juggle state standards, professional standards, district standards, and their representative tests, along with their own priorities within a subject area, to determine how to use standards effectively. This can be confusing and frustrating. Glatthorn's (1998) chapter in the *Curriculum Handbook* and Harris and Carr's *How to Use Standards in the Classroom* (1996) are helpful resources for clarifying how to work with standards.

There is some negativity toward the standards-based movement. It is seen as an anathema to creative teaching and learning (O'Neil & Tell, 1999; Wraga, 1999). This is indeed true if teaching with standards takes us back to a rigid traditional curriculum designed for the passive learner. It is also negative if curriculum alignment is seen as being geared to the standardized test, thereby insuring teaching to the test (Wraga, 1999).

Standards-based reform can be a setback to integrated approaches when standards are perceived as simply long lists of things to be covered. If teachers find themselves covering the curriculum by checking off a long list of standards, this could lead to a fragmented education, rather than meaningful lessons that are relevant to the learner.

I believe, however, that standards can bring about a very positive direction in education. Research demonstrates that schools do best when they pay attention to standards and performance (Fullan, 2000). A key to integration is alignment—not simply aligning the teacher to the test, but aligning the standards with assessment, reporting and learning experiences. When this occurs, the stage is set for effective schooling.

Skills-Based Standards

It is widely recognized that students today need to acquire skills that go far beyond the three Rs. They are expected to be productive citizens in a world where the information explosion is exponential and communication technology allows everyone, theoretically, equal access to that infor-mation. It is a world that requires a high level of technological skill in almost any career, as evidence in two reports. The U.S. Department of Labor published *What Work Requires of School: A SCANS Report for America 2000* (1991), and the Conference Board of Canada (1992) developed the *Employability Skills Profile*. Both reports outlined the skills neces-sary for the workplace of the 21st century. The reports, which were very similar, included skills such as

■ Basic skills, including reading, writing, arith-metic, listening, and speaking.
■ Thinking skills, including creative thinking, problem solving, reasoning, metacognition, and systems thinking.
■ Information skills, to include acquiring and eval-uating, organizing and maintaining, interpreting and communicating, and information processing on computers.
■ Technological skills.
■ Resource management.
■ Interpersonal skills, including team building, teaching, negotiating, and leadership.
■ Personal skills, including responsibility for oneself, self-esteem, and integrity.

These types of lists are being generated at many levels and are remarkably similar. A research team from nine nations, for example, came to consensus on characteristics a person will need to be a global citizen (Parker, Ninomiya, & Cogan, 1999). They include

■ Problem solving from a global perspective.
■ Working cooperatively.
■ Understanding, accepting, appreciating, and tolerating cultural differences.
■ Resolving problems nonviolently.
■ Critical thinking.
■ Participating in politics.

■ Changing one's lifestyle to protect the environment.
■ Defending human rights.

This shift in "what is worth knowing" is central to integrated curriculum. When the emphasis is on disciplinary content and procedures, it is more difficult to move out of preconceived boundaries. When interdisciplinary skills are considered as valuable as content, the door is open to plan for integrated curriculum. If students are learning problem-solving skills, for example, they can apply abilities that are interdisciplinary in nature, such as research skills. This frees them to explore a relevant problem in their community. The inquiry can then be deepened if students explore the problem through the lens of various disciplines. This approach allows for new insights that are often blocked by a disciplinary inquiry.

A popular tactic is for students to approach an issue from several perspectives, such as those of a historian, mathematician, and scientist (see, for example, Erickson, 1998, 1995; Lauritzen & Jaeger, 1998). Levy (1999) offers a framework for reflecting on experiences and designing projects. He has students consider the following questions (p. 73):

1. Mathematics: What is there to count and measure?
2. Science: What are the variables?
3. Reading: Have others had this experience? What did they learn?
4. Language and creative arts: What do I want to communicate to others about my experience?
5. Social studies: What have I learned about myself and my society?
6. Connections: How is this experience related to other experiences I have had?

Content Standards

A valid concern of educators is how to deal with the ever-increasing amount of content that can be included in the curriculum. The information explosion has made available too much material to ever properly cover most topics. To deal with this, teachers can organize learning to follow the structure of knowledge.

Facts are the lowest level of knowledge. Concepts—the broad, abstract categories that are universal and timeless, such as change, cause and effect, and probability—represent a higher level. Essential learning principles are a higher level of knowledge and are the big ideas that synthesize the learning. These principles state the relationship between two or more concepts. An example of a principle, or big idea, is "Technology changes our environment." The highest level of learning is theory.

How can the structure of knowledge direct our planning? Integrated curriculum has an organizing center; it can be a topic, theme, concept, process, issue, problem, event, novel, project, film, or song. Perkins (1989) urges planners to pick fertile themes. A fertile theme is broad, cuts across subject areas, and intrigues both the teacher and students. Curriculum specialist Rosemary Hunter, of Brock University, St. Catharines, Ontario, suggests, for example, that change, growth, and motion are rich concepts to use as themes.

The level of concepts and principles is a good starting point for choosing a curriculum theme, because they cut across subject areas. Cause and effect can be found, for example, in science, social studies, literature, and mathematics.

Teachers of interdisciplinary approaches are also interested in helping students attain higher-order thinking skills. Bloom's taxonomy of skills (1956) is still a useful tool for planning. Teachers need to teach the skills of application, analysis, synthesis, and evaluation. Erickson's work (1995, 1998) is particularly helpful in developing integrated curriculum using this concept-based approach, which includes process skills.

A good way to think about standards is as a pyramid (Figure 2.1). At the bottom are the facts and information that are content knowledge, or *knowing*. At this level, the achievement of standards is relatively easy to observe and measure through paper-and-pencil tests.

The second layer of the pyramid is much smaller and is composed of process or interdisciplinary skills such as communication, critical thinking, and technological literacy—*doing*. Given performance criteria, we can also observe and measure this level, although doing so is more complex. Many of these "skills" can be found in each discipline-based set of standards at the *doing* level. They are the higher-order thinking, or process, skills. Erickson (1995) defined process skills as internal student abilities that develop in sophistication over time—for example, reading and writing. At other times, they are referred to as the new basics.

The top of the pyramid refers to what we learn in school about who we are and what we value. This layer is about *being*—whether, for example, we demonstrate responsibility for ourselves and integrity in our actions.

The characteristics of the global citizen fit at the *being* level (Parker et al., 1999, pp. 117–145). The Singapore Ministry of Education acknowledges this layer of learning when it sets out to educate the whole child and includes as its outcomes that a child should

■ Have moral integrity.
■ Have care and concern for others.
■ Be enterprising and innovative.
■ Have an appreciation for aesthetics.
■ Be resilient and resolute (Bracey, 2000).

The *being* layer is much grayer and more difficult to measure and observe. In North America it is often dismissed as not being within the jurisdiction of the curriculum since it is the realm of values. Standards, however, are not value-free. Values are implicit in the higher-order thinking skills such as critical thinking, analysis, synthesis, judgment, and evaluation. It is best to be conscious of the basis for that standard. For example, analyzing and evaluating a local environmental problem will not be done with a value-free lens. Assumptions will be embedded in the analysis and evaluation.

My colleague Rosemary Hunter uses the be, know, and do categories with teachers who are planning curriculum with standards. A helpful hint she

FIGURE 2.1
The Standards Pyramid

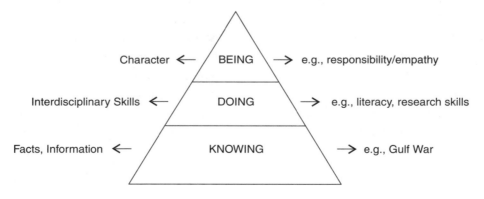

offers is to identify the standard's content by the nouns (know) and the skill by the verbs (do). The values (be) are implicit in the standard.

The *being* layer is very important to many teachers. For example, Mike McDonald, of the Grand Erie District School Board is certain that teaching compassion and empathy are critical regardless of what facts and knowledge are in the curriculum. Bob Ogilvie of the same school board adds that he believes we must instill beliefs that value the environment. Grade 5 teacher Janie Senko believes that integrated curriculum, properly delivered, helps students become responsible citizens—by listening to their opinions and by giving them the freedom to make choices and opportunities to solve problems and work together as team members. In the final analysis, students are also learning values from their teachers. What they do and don't do in the classroom speaks volumes—for in the ultimate analysis, we teach who we are, values and all (Drake, 1997).

Evaluation

In most jurisdictions, the initial response to issues of accountability has been a return to standardized testing. The results of this kind of testing are clear to the public. Many argue vehemently against standardized testing—in particular, high-stakes testing. They claim, and rightly so, that when teachers teach to these tests, students are robbed of other valuable learning experiences.

Schmoker (2000) points out that there are advantages to standardized testing. Dramatically improved performances in many school districts have resulted from a wide range of testing procedures, including standardized ones. From his perspective, standardized tests promote a common instructional focus and abandon ineffective teaching practices. He suggests that we work hard to bring all students to proficiency through the standardized

test. He also suggests that we should work toward an assessment system that combines standardized tests and alternatives.

As educators become more comfortable with using an integrated approach and standards, standardized tests seem to become less an issue for them. In part this is because they have found that students who learn in a context of integration achieve satisfactory results on tests, and also because teachers are learning strategies to deal with standardization. At the same time, there is a new policy direction, at least in Ontario, to change the shape of standardization to allow for the demonstration of thinking skills and abilities not shown on multiple-choice tests. This step is crucial to legitimizing interdisciplinary programs. Finally, there needs to be education of the general public about the legitimacy of alternative evaluation systems so that it becomes possible to move in this direction.

RECENT RESEARCH

New Ways to Understand Learning and Knowing

It is impossible to enter into a discussion about integrating curriculum without addressing some fundamental questions about how we learn, views of intelligence, and brain research. New research on learning suggests new ways of teaching. A broadened conception of intelligence, brain research, and a constructivist model of learning have all contributed to new ways to think about learning. These new understandings have, in turn, affected how we teach and how we conduct assessments. Innovative ways of teaching and assessing are connected to integrated curriculum. In part, this is because teachers who are willing to experiment with interdisciplinary approaches are the same teachers who are on the forefront of educational theory. And the application of these theories leads naturally to interdisciplinary approaches.

New Views of Intelligence

In traditional conceptions of education, intelligence or IQ was fixed at birth and could be measured on a pencil-and-paper test. The seminal work of Howard Gardner (1999, 1983) on multiple intelligences, or MI, has challenged this view and has had a dramatic impact on education. Gardner claims that schools traditionally teach to only two intelligences: linguistic and mathematical-logical. This indeed is the realm of the traditional IQ test. He suggests that there are at least six more intelligences: spatial, musical, interpersonal, intrapersonal, bodily kinesthetic, and naturalist. (He recently added the naturalist intelligence and is open to the addition of more.) He claims that when we include the other intelligences in teaching, students learn more fully.

Interestingly, Gardner rejects the notion of an integrated curriculum, arguing that the disciplines are still the best vehicle for learning (Scherer, 1999). Nevertheless, a wide variety of applications of MI are interdisciplinary in nature. The classic works of Armstrong (1993) and Lazear (1991) are good examples. When a teacher specifically includes, for example, bodily kinesthetic intelligence in a lesson, this can move the curriculum beyond physical education to such possibilities as a structured lab, using manipulatives and dance, and incorporating mime or creative dramatics (Bellanca, Chapman, & Swartz, 1994).

Other researchers have had an impact on conceptions of intelligence and how this should affect what happens in teaching. Goleman (1996) argues that emotional intelligence is crucial to success in life. Emotional intelligence involves such things as self-awareness, self-discipline, and empathy. These are life skills that fall under the umbrella of common essential learning and *being*. Integrated curriculum is an excellent way to address emotional intelligence, as teachers can cover content and move beyond it. Emotional intelligence

requires that time be spent for teaching and practicing the skills of reflection. Teachers can include such things as peer and self-assessment in group contexts, along with reflective journals, to begin to address emotional intelligence.

Brain Research

Very recently there have been a number of discoveries in brain research that educators have connected to the way humans learn (see, for example, Caine & Caine, 1997; Jensen, 1998; Sylwester, 1995). Some of the most relevant findings are that

■ We learn by making connections and thus creating meaning.
■ The more connections we can make to previous knowledge, the more we learn.
■ Emotions are critical to learning.
■ Our brains develop through interactions with the environment and others.
■ Learning is an active process.
■ We learn best in supportive but challenging environments.

These findings have direct implications for teaching from an interdisciplinary stance. Sylwester (1995) suggests that a thematic curriculum seems to develop a junglelike brain—one that demands a junglelike classroom, thriving on many sensory, cultural, and problem experiences connected to the real world. Such a classroom helps students find relationships between seemingly random facts and enduring understandings.

A number of brain-based approaches to teaching have emerged based on these principles. Working with a yearlong theme, Kovalik's model of integration (1994) focuses on meaningful content, an enriched environment, choice for students, time, and ongoing immediate feedback. Yearlong themes clearly must be fertile ones. Caine and Caine (1997) also offer ways in which principles from brain research connect to integrated curriculum. They stress the generation of deep meaning, complex authentic experiences, and active processing.

Bruer (1999) cautions us that brain-based research may not be all that educators are claiming. In spite of huge advances on the part of brain researchers, still little is understood about how the brain actually connects to learning. He claims that the recommendations emerging from brain-based education are, in reality, based on cognitive and constructivist models of learning that are firmly rooted in more than 30 years of psychological research.

Constructivism

Constructivism is based on psychology, philosophy, and anthropology, and rooted in the work of Piaget, Vygotsky, and Bruner. It first emerged in math and the sciences. Educators found it hard to explain how students who were taught a scientific concept still insisted that the misconceptions they had brought with them were correct. No matter how vigorous the evidence to the contrary, students hung onto their misconceptions!

This type of situation, repeated over and over, convinced many educators that students were not simply passive vessels absorbing knowledge. Rather, they constructed knowledge. Students came with previous experiences; new knowledge was assimilated or accommodated with this previous learning. A number of principles emerged from these initial insights (see, for example, Brooks & Brooks, 1993; Perkins, 1999):

■ Knowledge and understanding are socially constructed.
■ Knowledge is actively acquired.
■ Learners need to create or re-create knowledge for themselves.

These new understandings of learning came from somewhat different theoretical backgrounds. However, they all were alike enough to point to similar implications for teaching.

How Should We Teach?

Principles of teaching have emerged from the new understandings for learning. The five central tenets of constructivism help to create the picture (Brooks & Brooks, 1999):

1. Seeking and valuing the students' point of view.
2. Challenging student suppositions.
3. Developing relevant curriculum.
4. Structuring lessons around big ideas, not fragmented bits of information.
5. Making assessment part of the learning process.

Ultimately, a constructivist approach relates to students acquiring an understanding rather than simply memorizing and regurgitating facts. Constructivism is not just a toolbox of techniques. Windschitl (1999) points out that a constructivist classroom has a cultural system. The learning involves understanding gained by prolonged engagement with a topic; problem solving is the foundation of intellectual activity; and content is often integrated across subject areas. The classrooms of Geoff Suderman-Gladwell and Lindsey Stewart of Grand Erie District School Board illustrate a cultural system of constructivism.

Suderman-Gladwell (2000) paints the picture of his grade 6 constructivist classroom. He believes that "children will learn what they want to learn. My job is to help them want to learn what they need to know" (p. 1). He engages the students by focusing on their questions. Learning experiences are active. Who won the War of 1812? Instead of only reading about the war or hearing a lecture, the students take the roles of the Americans and the

British and replay the details of the war while demanding explanations from the other side. Debates take place naturally.

Suderman-Gladwell acts as a facilitator, offering key pieces of information to both sides. Students work together in small groups, since learning is a social activity. He allows choice in assignments that can be completed in the student's own time. Students are assessed on an ongoing basis so that they know explicitly that process is as important as content. Suderman-Gladwell values the learning style of all learners and creates a variety of tasks to allow for this. Sometimes he worries that his students talk too much and have too much freedom. In the final analysis, however, the students' response to his method of teaching assures him that he is on the right track.

In grade 1, Lindsey Stewart's (2000) students work independently, engage in discussions, ask and answer questions, and help their peers. Assessment is part of the daily activities and is embedded in the curriculum. She promotes an environment of mutual respect by giving the children the opportunity to create the classroom rules. She has regular class meetings. She models problem-solving strategies to help students deal with social conflicts. Intent on creating a meaningful curriculum, Stewart chooses to teach integrated units that cover standards from across the curriculum. The level of her students' development is important to her as she plans her predominantly active lessons. Students are encouraged to reflect on their own reasoning and share this in small groups. Stewart is delighted by the enthusiasm and love for learning her students have displayed and the quality of the final products they created.

Given this view of teaching and assessing, staying strictly within the boundaries of the disciplines is not necessarily practical. Real-life contexts pay little heed to artificial boundaries. Students will have acquired previous knowledge that is not neces-sarily discipline-bound. Their curiosities and questions will send them in new directions that may or may not be discipline-related. Structuring lessons around the big ideas that cut across disciplines is ultimately about making connections. Integrated curriculum is also essentially about making connections.

Aligning Teaching, Learning, and Assessing

The principles of learning should be aligned with how we teach and how we assess. Windschitl (1999) suggests several practices that fit the culture of a constructivist classroom. They include:

■ Students and teachers can negotiate criteria for evaluation.
■ Students and teachers together develop the criteria (rubrics) used for rigorous judgment.
■ Process skills are valued as well as product.
■ Students explain and defend their work.

An interesting way to think of aligning teaching and assessing is to begin with principles of learning. Given a principle of learning, how logically should we teach and assess? I have worked with many educators to discover if there are principles of teaching and assessment that can be derived from principles of learning. Teachers begin by sharing stories of both positive and negative learning experiences. Drawing from these stories, they develop a list of learning principles. This list always looks very similar to other groups who participate in the same exercise. The next step is to explore how a specific principle of learning can inform choices for teaching strategies, followed by what this learning principle means for assessment. For example, if people learn by doing, it follows that teaching strategies should involve active learning (doing), and the assessment should assess the doing (performance assessment). Figure 2.2 offers typical ideas of many educators who have participated in this activity.

FIGURE 2.2
Principles of Learning, Teaching, and Assessment

Learning		Teaching		Assessment
Learn by doing	→	Provide hands-on activities	→	Assess the doing, performance assessment
Choice	→	Offer choice	→	Choices in/with assessment
Relevant	→	Make activities personally relevant	→	Assessment should have meaning
Positive reinforcement	→	Offer a variety of positive reinforcements	→	Ongoing assessment should include constructive criticism and opportunity to redo
Supportive environment	→	Praise, learn from mistakes, take risks, offer constructive criticism	→	Assessment should include positives as well as negatives
Enjoyable, fun	→	Do fun activities	→	Assessment is a part of learning, but it can also be enjoyable
Challenging	→	Set high standards	→	Assessment should not be watered down but challenging to the level of student
Clear expectations	→	Teach explicit criteria for expectation	→	Assess specific criteria for expectations
Ongoing feedback	→	Provide ongoing feedback	→	Use ongoing assessment
Reflection by group and individual	→	Allow time for reflection	→	Use journals, discussion, quiet time
Learn by teaching	→	Teach others in class (e.g., jigsaw, tutoring, demonstration)	→	Assess the teaching performance of students
Metacognition	→	Use metacognition strategies	→	Assess metacognition
Variety of ways to learn	→	Use variety of teaching strategies	→	Use a variety of assessment tools (e.g., portfolios)
Modeling	→	Teacher walks the talk	→	Use teacher self-assessment and student evaluation of teacher

Source: Adapted from Drake, Susan M., *Creating integrated curriculums: Proven ways to increase learning*, p.157. Copyright 1998 by Corwin Press Inc. Reprinted by permission of publisher.

This section has set integrated curriculum into a context of tension between accountability and effective pedagogy. The tension is tangible. However, educators are finding ways to develop an integrated curriculum that is both accountable and taught according to the most effective learning principles.

WORKS CITED

Armstrong, T. (1993). *Seven kinds of smart: Identifying and developing your many intelligences.* New York: Plume.

Bellanca, J., Chapman, C., & Swartz, E. (1994). *Multiple assessments for multiple intelligences.* Palatine, IL: SkyLight.

Bloom, B. (1956). *A taxonomy of educational objectives.* (Handbook 1, Cognitive domain). New York: McKay.

Bracey, G. (2000). Coming of age of Singapore. *Phi Delta Kappan, 81*(7), 551–552.

Brooks, G., & Brooks, M. (1993). *In search of understanding: The case for constructivist classrooms.* Alexandria, VA: Association for Supervision and Curriculum Development.

Brooks, G., & Brooks, M. (1999). The courage to be constructivist. *Educational Leadership, 57*(3), 18–24.

Bruer, J. (1999). In search of brain-based education. *Phi Delta Kappan, 80*(9), 648–657.

Caine, R., & Caine, G. (1997). *Education on the edge of possibility.* Alexandria, VA: Association for Supervision and Curriculum Development.

Conference Board of Canada. (1992). *Employability skills profile: What are employers looking for?* (Brochure EE-F). Ottawa, Ontario: Author.

Czerniak, C. M., Weber, W. B., Sandmann, A., & Adhern, J. (1999). A literature review of science and mathematics integration. *School Science and Mathematics, 99*(8), 421–430.

Drake, S. M. (1997). Confronting the ultimate outcome: We teach who we are. In T. Jennings (Ed.), *Restructuring for integrated education* (pp. 39–51). Westport, CT: Bergin & Garvey Press.

Erickson, H. L. (1995). *Stirring the head, heart and soul: Redefining curriculum and instruction.* Thousand Oaks, CA: Corwin.

Erickson, H. L. (1998). *Concept-based curriculum and instruction: Teaching beyond the facts.* Thousand Oaks, CA: Corwin.

Fullan, M. (2000). The three stories of educational reform. *Phi Delta Kappan, 81*(8), 581–584.

Gardner, H. (1983). *Frames of mind: The theory of multiple intelligences.* New York: BasicBooks.

Gardner, H. (1999). *Intelligence reframed: Multiple intelligences for the 21st century.* New York: BasicBooks.

Glatthorn, A. A. (1998). *Planning and organizing for curriculum renewal.* (A chapter of the *Curriculum Handbook*). Alexandria, VA: Association for Supervision and Curriculum Development.

Goleman, D. (1996). *Emotional intelligence.* New York: Bantam Books.

Gregory, K. (1999). *The royal diaries: Cleopatra VII, daughter of the Nile, Egypt, 57 B.C.* New York: Scholastic.

Hargreaves, A., & Earl, L. (1990). *Rights of passage: A review of selected research about schooling in the transition years.* Toronto, Ontario: Ministry of Education.

Harris, D. E., & Carr, J. F. (1996). *How to use standards in the classroom.* Alexandria, VA: Association for Supervision and Curriculum Development.

Jensen, E. (1998). *Teaching with the brain in mind.* Alexandria, VA: Association for Supervision and Curriculum Development.

Kovalik, S. (1994). *ITI, the model: Integrated thematic instruction* (3rd ed.). Kent, WA: Books for Educators.

Lauritzen, C., & Jaeger, M. (1998). The transforming power of literature: "An afternoon in the stacks." *The New Advocate, 11*(3), 229–238.

Lazear, D. (1991). *Seven ways of knowing: Teaching for the multiple intelligences.* Palatine, IL: SkyLight.

Levy, S. (1999). To see the world in a grain of sand. *Educational Leadership, 57*(3), 70–75.

Ontario Ministry of Education (1993, 1995). *The Common Curriculum: Policies and Outcomes, Grades 1-9.* Toronto: Ministry of Education and Training, Government of Ontario.

O'Neil, J., & Tell, C. (1999). How students lose when 'tougher standards' win: A conversation with Alfie Kohn. *Educational Leadership, 57*(1), 18–22.

Parker, W. C., Ninomiya, A., & Cogan, J. (1999). Educating world citizens: Toward multinational curriculum development. *American Educational Research Journal, 36*(2), 117–145.

Perkins, D. (1989). Selecting fertile themes for integrated learning. In H. H. Jacobs (Ed.), *Interdisciplinary curriculum: Design and development* (pp. 67–76). Alexandria, VA: Association for Supervision and Curriculum Development.

Perkins, D. (1999). The many faces of constructivism. *Educational Leadership, 57*(3), 6–11.

Scherer, M. (1999). The understanding pathway: A conversation with Howard Gardner. *Educational Leadership, 57*(3), 12–16.

Schmoker, M. (2000). The results we want. *Educational Leadership, 57*(5), 62–65.

Scott, R. (1999, December). *Integrated curriculum model in a middle school.* Paper presented at the Ontario Educational Research Conference, Toronto, Ontario.

Stewart, L. (2000). *A constructivist classroom.* Unpublished paper.

Suderman-Gladwell, G. (2000). *Reinventing my classroom in a social constructivist vein.* Unpublished paper.

Sylwester, R. (1995). *A celebration of neurons: An educator's guide to the human brain.* Alexandria, VA: Association for Supervision and Curriculum Development.

U.S. Department of Labor, the Secretary's Commission on Achieving Necessary Skills (1991). *What work requires of school: A SCANS report for America 2000.* Washington, DC: Author.

Vars, G. (2000). News of NACC Members. *The Core Teacher, 50*(3).

Windschitl, M. (1999). A vision educators can put into practice: Portraying the constructivist classroom as a cultural system. *School Science and Mathematics, 99*(4), 189–196.

Wraga, W. G. (1999). The educational and political implications of curriculum alignment with standards-based reform. *Journal of Curriculum and Supervision, 13*(1), 26–34.

III. PRACTICAL STRATEGIES

PLANNING A STANDARDS-BASED CURRICULUM

Working with standards incorporates a fundamentally new approach to planning. Previously teachers were expected to begin planning with objectives to determine what they would teach to students. These objectives focused generally on content. Typically teachers would spend most of their time and energy selecting teaching activities they knew would appeal to students. The problem was that often the activities, although usually good, were not connected in any systematic way to the unit's goals or objectives. Evaluation strategies were selected last, often as an afterthought. Whether the lesson was learned was up to the student; the learning would be evaluated by a pencil-and-paper test.

In a standards-based process, teachers focus first on what students should know and do at the end of the learning experience. Over time, of course, they articulate what they want students to be like. Assessment and standards are inextricably linked, because teachers need to decide how they will require students to demonstrate their attainment of various standards. Only then can teachers begin to plan the instructional strategies or activities that will enable students to meet the standards. This process is known by such names as "mapping backward" or "designing down."

Figure 3.1 illustrates the shift from the traditional model to mapping backward or designing down. As portrayed here, the choice of the topic or theme for study emerges during this process. The topic is often embedded in the standards or local curriculum documents, or it can be based on student interests. Teachers begin reviewing relevant documents such as state or national standards and local curriculum guidelines. They select appropriate standards or results that students are expected to demonstrate at the end of the unit. Throughout the planning process they are to think like assessors (Wiggins & McTighe, 1998): What prerequisite skills and knowledge are needed? What assessment tools would be appropriate to measure attainment of the standards? Ideally assessment includes performance rather than only the students' capacity to memorize facts for a standardized or teacher test.

In the spirit of thinking like an assessor, teachers decide on a culminating activity. Rubrics with performance criteria are developed for the activity to ensure that students are meeting the standards. The next step is to decide what students will need to learn in order to complete the culminating activity successfully. Once this has been decided, learning experiences or subtasks can be created that give students opportunities for hands-on learning. The activities should connect directly to the general standards that lead to the final activity. In addition to content, *students must be taught the skills necessary to execute the culminating task.* For example, if they are expected to create a CD-ROM, they must learn the skills to do so.

In practice, it has been difficult for teachers to shift to mapping backward. For eight years I did training across North America using this model. I was often met with resistance—particularly from educators who had been "sent" unwillingly to the workshop. In hindsight, I realize that these teachers had no real understanding of what the shift really meant in practice and were not convinced that the result would be superior to the traditional planning method they were following. This shift in thinking is still difficult for teachers to make. However, there are now many teachers who experimented with the process until they understood it. These teachers generally find mapping backward an excellent way to improve learning in the classroom.

An example of mapping backward can be found in Figure 3.2. It shows an eight-step process that evolved from the work of two Ontario efforts at the elementary level. Both efforts were similar, and I

FIGURE 3.1
Curriculum Planning: Traditional vs. Designing Down

Traditional:

| topic/theme | → | objectives | → | teaching activities to teach content | → | evaluation |

Designing down:

| standards | → | topic/theme | → | culminating activity ↕ assessment | → | learning experiences to achieve standards ↕ assessment |

have streamlined them into one process for this chapter.

Mike McDonald of the Grand Erie District School Board headed up a curriculum team developing an integrated unit for grade 5. He was inspired by the work of teacher consultant Janet Rubas. In the other effort, Deb Pitblado and Jane Bennett from the Halton District School Board were part of the curriculum team, led by Ron Ballentine. They developed a combined grade 1 and 2 environmental unit.

The process is presented three times. Figure 3.2 is a brief synopsis of the steps. The section below, Walking Through the Process, provides a detailed explanation of each step. Applications are described in the section Applying the Models (see page 32).

WALKING THROUGH THE PROCESS

1. *Choose standards from two or more subject areas that are general in nature. Do not choose more than three from any subject. This process will give a general direction for the topic of study.*

Given the vast range of standards, teachers must evaluate what is most important to learn. Often curriculum documents do this through defini-

tions of standards. Ontario offers general or broad-based standards along with specific ones for each subject area. Vermont's Framework of Standards and Learning Opportunities features the Vital Results—standards that are not content-specific and are interdisciplinary.

The general or overall standards do not dictate the specific content to be explored; they involve process skills and concepts or learning principles that can be taught in many contexts. The overall standards are considered the most important things to be learned. For example, the student will

■ Identify distinguishing features of urban and rural communities (social studies).
■ Evaluate data and draw conclusions from data (math).
■ Express and respond to ideas and opinions concretely (language arts).
■ Demonstrate an understanding of some of the principles involved in the structure of works in drama and dance.

More specific standards may or may not determine the content area; these differ in different curriculum documents. For example, the *Ontario Curriculum Grades 1–8 Science*, a document put out by the Ontario Ministry of Education (1997) is very prescriptive and content-driven in comparison with other subject areas. The theme or topic is dictated by these standards. For example, an overall standard in this document calls on the student to demonstrate an understanding of the characteristics and properties of light and sound (science and technology).

It is crucial to begin this process by selecting only a few of the most general standards. These act

as an umbrella for the whole unit. The more standards initially chosen, the more difficult it is to integrate in a natural way. In reality, teachers find that most of the more specific standards are embedded in and support the general ones. When they plan using general standards to create learning experiences, they find they have also covered one or two specific standards. As a natural consequence, many more specific standards can be identified as students move through the unit.

For example, the more general science standard mentioned previously can be supported by the specific standards drawn from the following topics:

- Natural and artificial light sources
- Behavior and basic characteristics of light
- Color as a property of light
- Sounds as caused by vibrations
- Human ear design
- Range of sounds and frequency

The topic or theme will likely emerge during the first three steps of the process. There are many ways to determine a topic for study. It should appeal to students' genuine interests and needs. Possible community resources should be considered. Many advocate that students actually be included in a large part of the planning process (see, for example, Beane, 1997; Stevenson & Carr, 1993). Students can become familiar with standards in the same way that teachers must. When students learn to evaluate themselves through standards and rubrics, the learning tends to be enhanced.

2. Develop a "learning bridge" that connects the standards selected. These may include what students will know (concepts and principles), do (process skills), and be (affective component).

The learning bridge needs to connect the standards at a level beyond the disciplines. Concepts and principles (knowing) and process skills (doing)

FIGURE 3.2
A Standards-Based Interdisciplinary Curriculum Planning Process

The topic of the unit will likely emerge during the process of working through the first three steps. However, there are many ways to determine a topic for study including student interests and needs or community resources. *The important thing is that the standards, assessment, and instructional strategies are aligned.* These steps are not necessarily linear but do begin by examining standards and local curriculum guidelines.

1. Choose one to three standards from two or more subject areas that are general and broad-based in nature.

2. Develop a "learning bridge" that connects the standards selected. These may include what students will know (concepts and principles), do (process skills), and be (affective component).

3. Create a standards-based web by reorganizing standards into clusters that fit together naturally to create new cross-disciplinary categories.

4. Create focus questions. Blend focus questions to create Big Questions to guide unit.

5. Brainstorm with students what they already know about the Big Questions.

6. Decide on a culminating task.

7. Develop a grade-specific assessment rubric for the culminating task.

8. Create a subset of learning experiences that lead to the culminating activity.

---

cut across the curriculum. In addition, how do we want the students to act (being) when they are engaged in the curriculum tasks? Although this aspect is difficult to measure and is controversial in some states, it still needs to be considered. Acting in democratic ways, for example, is often proclaimed as a way we want students to be.

The learning bridge should focus on "understandings" that students are to attain by the end of the unit. Understanding involves abstract and conceptual ideas that are not necessarily immediately apparent or explicit (Wiggins & McTighe, 1998). Understanding is demonstrated by being able to apply both knowledge and skill in a real-life context. Students may know something but not really understand it. Wiggins and McTighe offer the example of grade 8 students who were presented with the question, "How many buses does the army need to transport 1,128 soldiers if each bus holds 36 soldiers?" Almost one-third of the students answered 31 with "a remainder of 12," illustrating a true lack of understanding.

3. *Create a standards-based web by reorganizing standards into clusters that fit together naturally and create new cross-disciplinary categories.*

At this point the theme for the unit becomes clear, and standards can be reorganized to fit certain topics within the theme. It is helpful to create this web as a visual aid for the process. Figure 3.3 offers an example of a standards-based web.

4. *Create focus questions based on concepts embedded in standards.*

The focus questions will guide the learning experiences leading to the culminating activity. Carefully crafted questions are important to ensure that students have the opportunity for understanding. In this approach the questions are generated from the standards.

What concepts do you want students to learn? What principles do you want them to take with

them from the classroom? Once these are identified, focus questions can be developed.

A second step is to blend focus questions to create Big Questions that guide the entire unit; general standards will be embedded into these.

Several different learning experiences may address a Big Question. These questions guide the entire unit and act as umbrellas for the focus questions. They should be two to five questions that are general in nature, connected to several disciplines and in a logical framework (Jacobs, 1989). The questions serve to limit the topic under study and focus on what is most important to learn. Alternatively, they can be generated with students during Step 5. Many teachers post them at the front of the class during the unit so students are constantly aware of what is important to learn.

5. *Brainstorm with students to draw out what they already know about the Big Questions. Develop curriculum considering prior knowledge, standards, and concepts that are to be taught.*

A popular strategy teachers use for this step is called K-W-L, for the three categories: know, want to know, and learn. Students respond to the following three questions:

    a. What do you already know?
    b. What do you need to know?
    c. How will you know when we have learned it?

6. *Decide on a culminating task to end the unit that incorporates standards, concepts, process skills, and students' prior knowledge.*

The culminating activity puts it all together, and students are introduced to this expectation at the beginning of a unit. It is often performance-based, observable, and measurable. It may involve an exhibition, a major presentation, or the development of a model. Holding a fair, putting on a drama, making a presentation to a local council, and inventing, developing, and marketing a product are

FIGURE 3.3
A Standards-Based Web

UNDERSTANDING THE BODY

Science and Technology
■ Demonstrate understanding of the structure and function of the respiratory, circulatory, digestive, excretory, and nervous systems.

■ Investigate the structure and function of the major organs of the respiratory, circulatory, digestive, excretory, and nervous systems.

Visual Art
■ Define the elements of design (color, line, shape, form, space, texture) and use them in a way that is appropriate for this grade when producing and responding to works of art.

Language
■ Identify various types of media works and some techniques used in them.
■ Analyze media work.
■ Speak clearly when making presentations.
■ Communicate ideas and information for a variety of purposes (e.g. to present and support a viewpoint) and to specific audiences.

BODY IMAGE

Physical and Health Education
■ Analyze information that has an impact on healthy eating practices (e.g. food labels, food guides, care-of-teeth brochures).

Visual Art
■ Describe their interpretation of a variety of art works, basing their interpretation on evidence from the works (especially on ways in which an artist has used the elements of design to clarify meaning) and on their own knowledge and experience.

Language
■ Analyze media work.

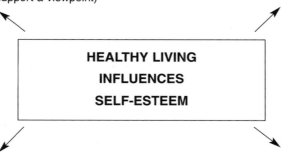

PEER PRESSURE

Physical and Health Education
■ Describe physical, emotional, and interpersonal changes associated with puberty.

Language
■ Identify various types of media works and some techniques used in them.
■ Use tone of voice, gestures, and other nonverbal clues to help clarify meaning.
■ Speak clearly when making presentations.

SELF-ESTEEM

Visual Art
■ Produce two- and three-dimensional works of art that communicate a range of ideas (thoughts, feelings, experiences) for specific purposes and to specific audiences.

Physical and Health Education
■ Demonstrate factors that contribute to good health.

Language
■ Contribute and work consecutively in groups.

Source: Adapted from the work of Linda Hedley, Nancy Rose, Shirley Thompson, and Mike McDonald of Grand Erie District School Board, Ontario.

typical of culminating activities. The activity should be connected to the focus questions and the Big Questions that guide the unit. It also should be connected to the standards selected. To demonstrate understanding (to show what students know and can do), the task should be complex, situated in an authentic context, and evaluated in ways that include both content and process.

7. *Develop a grade-specific assessment rubric for the culminating task.*

Rubrics include both content and process and assess various levels of competency (for example, levels 1-4). They need to match the standards initially selected. And they must be comprehensive of what a student must know and do to complete the culminating task. Rubrics are often developed with students, and that process increases their awareness of the criteria.

8. *Create a subset of learning experiences that lead to the culminating activity. These will emerge from the reclustering of standards in Step 3. For each subset identify*

■ Focus questions.
■ Standards—more specific standards that support the general ones can usually be added here.
■ The know, do, and be components (content, process, and affective).
■ Assessment tools.
■ Teaching and learning activities (instructional strategies).
■ Grouping.
■ Modification strategies.
■ Resources.

APPLYING THE MODELS

Super Systems: An Inner Journey

The following application has been adapted from the work of Linda Hedley, Nancy Rose, Shirley Thompson, and Mike McDonald of Grand Erie District School Board, Ontario. They began the process over dinner by discussing their individual views of what was important for a grade 5 student to know, do, and be by the end of the year. They were given release time for two full days for planning. Team members met six more times after school to write and review their work. From the first dinner, group members agreed that self-awareness and self-esteem were most important to teach their students. Based on their knowledge of the curriculum, they selected the subject areas that seemed to complement this direction. The topic emerged because they were concerned that the grade 5 students were already worried about their bodies, and some were on diets.

Step 1: *Choose standards from two or more subject areas that are general in nature. Do not choose more than three from any subject. They will give a general direction for the topic of study.*

All grade 5 general standards in selected subject areas were photocopied and reviewed. The standards selected were put into the following clusters:

SCIENCE AND TECHNOLOGY
■ Demonstrate understanding of the structure and function of the respiratory, circulatory, digestive, excretory, and nervous systems.
■ Investigate the structure and function of the major organs of the respiratory, circulatory, digestive, excretory, and nervous systems.

PHYSICAL AND HEALTH EDUCATION
■ Analyze information that has an impact on healthy eating practices—for example, food labels, food guides, and care-of-teeth brochures.
■ Describe physical, emotional, and interpersonal changes associated with puberty.

■ Demonstrate factors that contribute to good health.

THE ARTS
Visual Art
■ Define the elements of design—including color, line, shape, form, space, and texture—and use them in a way that is appropriate for this grade when producing and responding to works of art.
■ Describe students' interpretation of a variety of artworks, basing it on evidence from the works, especially on ways in which an artist has used the elements of design to clarify meaning, and on students' own knowledge and experience.
■ Produce two- and three-dimensional works of art that communicate a range of ideas—thoughts, feelings, and experiences—for specific purposes and to specific audiences.

Drama
■ Solve problems presented through drama and dance, working in large and small groups and using various strategies.

LANGUAGE
■ Identify various types of media works and some techniques used in them.
■ Analyze media work.
■ Speak clearly when making presentations.
■ Communicate ideas and information for a variety of purposes—for example, to present and support a viewpoint—and to specific audiences.
■ Use tone of voice, gestures, and other nonverbal clues to help clarify meaning.

Step 2: *Develop a "learning bridge" that connects the standards selected. These may include what students will know (concepts and principles), do (process skills), and be (affective component).*

Given the initial discussions, the team was able to quickly articulate what they wanted students

to know, do, and be. The following became the learning bridges.

KNOW
■ Healthy living (concept).
■ Self-esteem (concept).
■ Healthy living influences self-esteem (principle).

DO
■ Presentation skills
■ Writing skills
■ Visual art skills

BE
■ Demonstrate positive self-esteem.
■ Demonstrate respect for others.
■ Choose healthy living habits.

Step 3: *Create a standards-based web by reorganizing standards into clusters that fit together naturally and create new cross-disciplinary categories. An example of this is provided in Figure 3.3 (page 31).*

The team broke into pairs. The standards were cut up and reorganized into interdisciplinary clusters that each pair deemed represented actual life experiences familiar to most students. The pair groups then compared notes and collaboratively decided upon the clusters that they identified as potential learning experiences or subtasks. Standards that didn't fit were discarded at this point. A standards-based web was created from these new clusters (see Figure 3.3).

Step 4: *Create focus questions based on standards and concepts embedded in standards.*

Focus questions were created by reworking the standards; they were the foundation for relevant questions. Big Questions were constructed to help students and teachers see the direction of the unit and what was important to know.

FOCUS QUESTIONS
■ What are the structures and functions of the body systems and their major organs?
■ What are the physical, emotional, and interpersonal changes that happen at puberty?
■ How does peer pressure affect behavior?
■ How do art and media influence self-esteem?
■ How does knowledge of food and eating habits relate to how we live?
■ How does the concept of beauty relate to healthy living?
■ What factors contribute to good health?

A second step is to blend focus questions to create Big Questions to guide the unit.

BIG QUESTIONS
■ How does healthy living relate to our major organs and body systems?
■ What factors affect self-esteem?
■ How can we boost self-esteem?

Step 5: *Brainstorm with students about what they already know about the Big Questions. Develop curriculum considering prior knowledge, and expectations and concepts that are to be taught.*

The K-W-L strategy works well here. The team did not actually do this step but agreed that teachers would do this in the future with each unique group of students. This procedure will then determine the direction of the curriculum and may indeed shift the details offered in the next steps.

Step 6: *Decide on a culminating task to end the unit that incorporates standards, concepts, process skills, and students' prior knowledge.*

The following performance task was created considering the alignment of assessment with standards:

Your group has been granted a booth at the Health Fair. The slogan for the fair is, "Healthy living develops from an understanding of the human body, body image, peer pressure, and self-esteem." Your task is to convince the 6th grades and the general public who will attend the fair that this slogan is true. You will have a 15-minute time slot in which to present a docudrama to convince them. Allow time for questions from the audience. There will be rotating audiences (of no more than 10 people per group); you will repeat your presentation five times.

Working in your group, write a docudrama that supports the slogan for the health fair. You should include examples of the impact of peer pressure, and how the body image affects self-esteem. What are healthy living habits? You need at least 3 examples from the media to prove your points. Include your visual display of how a body system operates that demonstrates your application of art techniques.

You will be assessed on your written docudrama, your presentation skills, the completeness of the information you present, and your ability to answer the questions asked.

Step 7: *Develop a grade-specific assessment rubric for the culminating task.*

The team discussed what rubrics were necessary to give students to prepare them for assessment. (Alternatively, students can create rubrics with the teachers or each other.) The rubrics include performance criteria for

■ Completeness of the content of the docudrama.

■ Quality of writing for the docudrama (persuasive writing).

■ Use of examples from media to support the argument.

■ Use of visual art techniques with visual display of the body.

■ Dramatic and presentation skills (persuasive performance).

Step 8: *Create a subset of learning experiences that lead to the culminating activity. These will emerge from the reclustering of standards in Step 3. For each subset identify*

■ Focus questions.

■ Standards—as the learning activities unfold, more specific standards can usually be added to the more general ones.

■ The know, do, and be—content, process, and affective—components.

■ Assessment tools.

■ Teaching and learning activities.

■ Modification strategies.

■ Resources.

The team now turned to the learning experiences or subtasks they had created in Step 3 when they reclustered the standards. They had created four learning experiences. For each one, they repeated Steps 4 to 8 of the process. At this point more specific standards from the subject area documents were added. Pedagogical concerns were considered, such as groupings of students and modifications for special students. At all times, it was key that each learning experience connected to the goals of the larger unit, the standards, and the culminating assessment.

Problem-Based Learning

The steps for developing an interdisciplinary unit using problem-based learning, as described on page 38, are

■ Brainstorm for an ill-structured problem of interest to the students. Alternatively, give the students a real-life context and have them select issues or problems within that to explore.

■ Formalize the problem or scenario.

■ Decide on the "standards" that students will demonstrate that they meet by the end of the unit; this usually consists of the operations involved in solving the problem. Concepts and principles may also be included, but they are dependent on the nature of the problem.

■ Decide on ongoing assessment and a significant culminating activity that will demonstrate meeting the standards.

■ Create rubrics for demonstrating these skills by creating the required products.

■ Introduce students to the project through an initial session.

■ Introduce students to expectations for the course using accompanying rubrics.

■ Have students hand in a formal proposal for their problem solving.

■ Facilitate independent group study. The process requires research.

■ Design a solution.

■ Include a group presentation to an authentic audience.

■ Ask students to demonstrate learning in the culminating activity.

Example of Learning Experiences Subset
The following activities, focusing on peer pressure, led to the culminating task.

FOCUS QUESTIONS
■ How does peer pressure affect behavior?
■ How do art and media contribute to self-esteem?

STANDARDS
General Standards
PHYSICAL AND HEALTH EDUCATION
■ Describe physical, emotional, and interpersonal changes associated with puberty.

LANGUAGE
■ Identify various types of media works and some techniques used in them.
■ Use tone of voice, gestures, and other nonverbal clues to help clarify meaning.
■ Speak clearly when making presentations.

More Specific Standards Covered
■ Apply strategies to deal with threats to personal safety—for example, in response to harassment—and to prevent injury, for example, from physical assault.
■ Identify the influences—media, peers, and family, for instance—affecting alcohol use, along with the effects and legalities of alcohol use and healthy alternatives.
■ Identify various types of media works and some of the techniques used in them.
■ Use the conventions of oral language—for example, sentence structure—and of various media, as appropriate to grade level.
■ Express and respond to ideas and opinions concisely, clearly, and appropriately.

TEACHING AND LEARNING ACTIVITIES
Lesson 1
The teacher gives a different index card to triads of students. On each card is written a scenario of a negative situation with body image or peer pressure. For example, one card describes a situation in which a grade 4 girl is on a strict diet because some of her classmates teased her and called her "fat" in the schoolyard. Students role-play the situation.

As a class, the students brainstorm for positive strategies to deal with the situation. Students choose one solution and repeat the role-playing with a new ending. This can be followed by more discussion on possible negative impacts of body image and peer pressure and positive strategies to deal with the negatives (for example, peer pressure to smoke). Students summarize their knowledge by completing a T chart that lists negative impacts and positive strategies.

Lesson 2
In pairs, students then select negative impacts and positive strategies to create a collage illustrating their selection. The teacher reviews methods of creating effective collages and montages. Exemplars of interesting collages can be examined. Students combine their own reflections, drawings, words, and magazine pictures to create a collage that demonstrates both negative impacts and positive strategies.

Know—Content
■ Concept of peer pressure.
■ Concept of body image.
■ Possible negative impacts of peer pressure and body image on self-esteem.
■ Positive ways to handle negative impacts.

Do—Process skills
- Brainstorming
- Issue-based analysis
- Problem posing
- Problem solving
- Role-playing
- Techniques for creating a collage

Be—Affective domain
- Be respectful of others.

INSTRUCTIONAL STRATEGIES: EXPERIENTIAL AND INTERACTIVE

Assessment
Performance Tasks

(Source: Lynette Fast, Brock University, St. Catharines, Ontario)

Students will compare the visual characteristics of professional artworks (collages and other two-dimensional pictures) that show negative and positive interactions and moods. Students will use cut and torn papers to complete a two-dimensional collage on a Bristol board support that is divided vertically, horizontally, or diagonally. Their selection of colors, shapes, and lines for the two sections will demonstrate ideational and visual contrast—that is, negative and positive interpersonal relationships through paper sizes, edges, and values (light and dark), along with their placement on the page. The artworks may be narrative or expressionistic.

Students will orally explain the reasons for their choices in portraying contrasts and will participate in a culminating large-group critique of collages by members of the class.

Assessment Criteria

A) Demonstration of knowledge of collage as an art form and of design terms in the art product and in oral communication; and

B) Demonstration of an analysis of the problem for the selection and placement of materials for effective communication.

GROUPINGS
- Whole class
- Group work
- Individual work

ADAPTATIONS
- Modify expectations of finished collage.
- Offer individual assistance with recording impacts and strategies.
- Encourage reticent students to participate in discussion.
- Facilitate further research for interested students.

RESOURCES
- Index cards prepared with scenarios.
- Magazines, papers, and art supplies for collages.
- Exemplars for collages.

Final Step. *Reflection on the unit*

The group had been influenced by the concept of thinking like an assessor. They reviewed the document they had created by comparing it to their goals at the beginning and checking that the standards, culminating activity, assessment, and learning experiences were aligned. They were also aware of the need for both the teacher and students to evaluate the unit when it was being taught. What worked? What should be changed for another time? This reflection would be an ongoing process for them.

Standards-Based Interdisciplinary Model: Problem-Based Learning

Another possibility for developing interdisciplinary units is problem-based learning. This approach is similar to the concept-based model, but it is not driven by specific content or concepts included in curriculum standards. Rather this model relies on solving a problem—often one found in a real-life context. The process skills involved in solving the problem are the "learning bridge." Research skills are a typical example. The standards to be addressed, then, are the cross-disciplinary process skills that can be found in each subject area's document of standards. Clearly, knowledge is also important in this context. The teacher needs to be particularly careful in identifying the central concepts and principles to be learned.

The Millennium Project

The Millennium Project was created by the Assessment Training Consortium. It involved five Ontario school boards (districts): Durham, Halton, Lakehead, Toronto, and Waterloo. These boards are responsible for more than 500,000 students. Chaired by Leo Plue of the Durham District School Board, the Millennium Project was seen as a vital link to secondary school reform in Ontario. The project coupled problem-based learning with standards-based performance assessment (Schmidt, M., & Plue, L., 2000). It was generic enough for the five school boards to apply in different ways, yet it still provided opportunities for students to demonstrate the essential knowledge, skills, and work habits they will need to be successful and responsible citizens in the 21st century.

The purpose of the project was to facilitate students' demonstration of cross-curricular skills. The skills were evaluated by rubrics developed by the consortium and were independent of individual projects and subject areas. Thus they were generic, as follows:

- Research
- Data collection and manipulation
- Written oral and visual communication
- Individual and collaborative working strategies
- Problem solving
- Numeracy, science, and technology
- Reflection and self-assessment

A problem acted as the starting point for students. This was the learning bridge. One key element of the project was that once students had been introduced to the problem and the process, it was largely fulfilled through independent work. The problem was intended to be an ill-structured one that was messy and complex and did not have one "right" answer. At most schools, the students were given a problem devised by the teachers at the school. Students worked together in groups.

The products for assessment were also suggested for all projects. These included such things as a formal proposal for solving the problem, a work log, a written report, an oral report, and an individual defense. An example of the formal proposal (Figure 3.7 on page 46) and a sample rubric for data collection (Figure 3.6 on page 43) are provided.

The goal of the project was to have all 11th grades in all consortium schools engaged in this curriculum by the fall of 2001. Meanwhile, a number of pilot projects have taken place, each of which has applied the "formula" a little differently to adapt to their unique contexts. Detailed examples of how the Millennium Project was implemented at Iroquois Ridge and Grand River Collegiate Institute are found in the Curriculum Integration in Practice section. A good illustration of how this model was used is offered in Figure 3.4.

The examples show two routes to interdisciplinary curriculum. Although the first example was conducted at the elementary level and the other was at the secondary level, both could be applied at

FIGURE 3.4
Durham District School Board

BACKGROUND

Title of Task: DISASTER!　　　　**Grade Level:** 11　　　　**Time Frame:** Equivalent of 25 hours

Curriculum areas: Mandatory - Math; Science; Technology; English // Other subjects can be integrated

Developed by:

Port Perry High School	Sinclair Secondary School
School Rep: Carolyn Scheffield	Board Rep: Susan Jones
Charles Wyezkowski	School Rep: Mike Clayton
Dennis Schilling	Jennifer Jenkins
Glen Rideout	Sarah Young
Bill Walters	

THE TASK

A disaster has hit Durham Region. Your consulting firm has learned a great deal from the aftermath of the disaster. Your group must develop and present a feasible community disaster plan to the Regional Council. Your plan must be supported by all the relevant data about this disaster.

Choosing Your Disaster:

From the chart below, choose one scenario from each box. This will be the disaster that your group deals with.

Type of Disaster	Time Frame		Location
	Occurrence Time	**Warning Time**	
Medical	Seconds	Seconds	Rural Durham Region
Natural Geographical	Minutes	Minutes	Urban Durham Region
Natural Environmental	Hours	Hours	Entire area of Durham Region
Computer/Technological	Days	Days	
Man-Made Environmental	A season	A season	
Man-Made Geographical	Years	Years	

A file will be given to each group with background information about the chosen disaster. Your group is expected to deal with the following information, making use of the math, science, English, and technological skills that you have. You can also integrate other subjects into your project if you wish.

Casualties	Statistics	Money Issues
State of Damage	Destruction of Infrastructure	Community Support

Process	**Product**
WORK IN PROGRESS BINDER (1 PER GROUP) Includes data collection; group reflection; group feedback sheets; group responsibilities.	WRITTEN REPORT (1 PER GROUP) Must include a breakdown of the group members and the workload; conclusions; graphs; etc.
JOURNAL/LOG BOOK (1 PER STUDENT) Includes personal reflection; personal feedback sheets; self-evaluation sheets; personal responsibilities.	PRESENTATION (1 PER GROUP) 1. ORAL 2. TECHNOLOGICAL 3. CREATIVE
FORMAL PROPOSAL (1 PER GROUP) Outlines the hypothesis; the problems to solve; potential avenues to explore; potential methods of presentation; subjects that are represented by the group members; how technology will be included; etc.	4. VISUAL Must include components from all represented subjects; must cover the content of the written report; must explain how the end results varied from the original proposal, and why; must address solutions and conclusions to the problem and hypothesis.
	ORAL DEFENSE Each group member must be able to answer questions from the assessor.

either level. As well, both begin with standards and connect knowledge from two or more subject areas.

CURRICULUM INTEGRATION IN PRACTICE

This section will focus on seven examples of integrated curriculum as it is successfully being implemented in classrooms today. To explore these sites, I interviewed key players in person or on the telephone. Those involved often supplemented this approach with written information to explain their programs in depth.

We begin with examples of one teacher in one classroom (outdoor education, narrative curriculum, or environmental science) and move on to efforts that increase in complexity. Two secondary examples of the Millennium Project are offered (one with three teachers and the second with 60). The more complex examples include an arts project that involves six sites, 20,000 students and 900 teachers. Finally, the Alpha Program is explored; this is a fully integrated multiage program for grades 6, 7, and 8.

Outdoor Education

A number of integrated programs have been successfully developed revolving around outdoor education. In 2000 there were 30 successful programs in Ontario (Russell & Burton, 2000). Detailed information on these programs, and Mike Elrick's below, are available from Bob Henderson, of McMaster University in Hamilton.

Mike Elrick, of Centennial Collegiate and Vocational Institute, Guelph, Ontario, is in the sixth year of teaching an integrated course. He has 24 grade 11 students who take the Community Environmental Leadership Program during the winter semester. The program costs each student $400.00. Each day for the five months of the program, they take a bus to an off-campus site. Here they take four credits—environmental science, environmental geography, personal life management (family studies), and outdoor education.

The premise guiding program delivery is that the knowledge of different subject areas overlaps; nothing is learned in isolation. As a result, students may take one week of outdoor education, followed by two weeks of environmental geography and science. However, there will be overlap into other areas during those weeks. For example, if students go on a canoe trip, they are learning skills in outdoor education, such as canoeing, as well as communication and problem-solving skills found in the standards for outdoor education and family studies. Learning about food and nutrition can be found in the family studies.

During the semester, students complete five units:

1. Community building
2. Wilderness winter camp experience
3. Life in habitat
4. Teaching the Earth Keeper program to grade 5 students
5. Bioregions—exploring their own region

For Elrick, the integrated program is a powerful tool. He has been surprised by what he has learned from teaching this course for six years: "The concept of community and friendship is of central importance. We need to treat each other with respect, tolerance, and love. These are the same lessons that we must learn in relating to the natural world. If we can't build this community, we will not be able to take care of the earth, either."

The students in Elrick's class feel free to be themselves and accept others. They are a community that does not, for example, judge someone on what they might wear. They are comfortable with who they are and therefore are free to think about how to live on the planet. This course takes students into the realm of being while also dealing with knowing and doing.

Non-College-Bound Environmental Science

How could Sharon DeFrees, of Baker High School in Baker City, Oregon, motivate her senior students who were taking environmental science only to meet graduation requirements and were not going on to university? Each year she had the students transform the wrestling room into a specific environment. One year, for example, it became an interactive rain forest with three separate regions. Students planned, developed, and carried out the project. They were divided into groups and assumed responsibility for an area. Research included such things as climate, people, soil, and environmental issues. After the initial research, students had to decide what was important to be included in their region of the diorama. Then they had to draw it and decide where everything should go. Students, for example, made trees, insects, and birds representative of their region. Art skills were crucial. Sound effects were also included. The culminating activity was to give a guided tour of the rain forest to students in kindergarten through 5th grade. To prepare the elementary students, they created a typed book outlining their research that the children read before coming on the tour. This was a very popular event for the elementary students.

DeFrees reports that they worked very hard during the project and that it meant a lot to the senior students. After the project, when she would often see them in the community, they would remind her of their enjoyment. They learned research, art, presentation, and expository writing skills, along with knowledge about the rain forest. What struck DeFrees was what they learned outside of the curriculum requirements. They were extremely creative—more creative than the advanced students she teaches. She hypothesized that this was because these students did not plan to go on to college and therefore did not perceive the same pressures as more academically oriented

students did. And they were extremely resourceful in a project without a budget. They got donations for bark chips from a local business, borrowed a pump for the fountain, and adapted trees that would later be used in forestry class.

Students were evaluated by their participation. Each day they would record in their groups what they planned to do and what would be done the next day. This kept everyone busy and accountable. DeFrees believes the keys to the program's success were the clear specifications and timelines that students were given at the beginning.

Learning Through Story: The Narrative Curriculum

A story is an excellent vehicle to develop integrated curriculum for elementary students. It is developed in *Integrating Learning Through Story: The Narrative Curriculum* (Lauritzen & Jaeger, 1997). The narrative curriculum begins and ends with a story. The curriculum is grounded in the belief that humans make meaning through story and that learning generated from stories fosters deep understanding and is long remembered. To begin, a story is read, students generate questions from the story, and they develop explorations to answer their own questions. There is a repetitive nature to the experience as students return again and again to the story.

The focus is usually on science and language arts, but many other disciplines are included. The focus comes from the goals of the curriculum, the questions the children generate, and the disciplinary heuristics that inform the explorations. The language curriculum is always involved because language is needed for communication. Science per se will not always be involved in the story, but scientific thinking will be brought into the curriculum. Explorations are created to encourage students to be critical and creative thinkers, collaborators and problem solvers. A central component is that students are given opportunities to explore their own natural sense of wonder.

The students in a 3rd grade class, for instance, read *Chicken Sunday* (Polacco, 1992), a story of cross-cultural trust and friendship (Lauritzen & Jaeger, 1998). Questions were generated collaboratively with the teacher. Explorations were designed and executed, for example, creating a mixed media art project, performing a creative dance, and painting repetitive patterns on eggs. During explorations, students were encouraged to think and work like disciplinary experts—for example, scientist, mathematician, artist, or historian. They also dramatized solving problems in social situations. In the culminating activity, the story was reread and the results of the explorations were presented. When the author had used mixed media, the students created their own mixed media pieces; they sang their version of the music in the story; and they sampled the Southern cooking that had been reconstructed from the meal in the story.

An observer of the culminating activity noted: "It was a complete and total sensory experience— the smells, the sounds, the visual stimuli. . . . It was 90 minutes of joyful engagement. The word for it is 'ecstasy,' and I don't use the word often." (Lauritzen & Jaeger, 1998). This is a great testimonial for the power of story and the possibilities of the narrative curriculum.

**The Millennium Project—
Biology and Geography**

Stuart Miller, of Iroquois Ridge High School, Halton District School Board, Ontario, led the Millennium Project. It was officially conducted in his and Donna Taylor's grade 11 biology classes and Rob McDowell's grade 11 geography class. Students completed the project over two weeks during 80-minute classes. A letter of permission was sent to the parents introducing the Millennium Project and explaining that the students would be involved in

independent study and therefore might be out of the school during class time.

The first session lasted a full day. Students were given a scenario. Their school was set in a location where forest had been cut down to make way for large upper-middle-class homes. Was this development good? If not, why? The teachers wanted students to understand the concept of complexity and the principle that "real-life issues can be multifaceted and complex." They developed a framework within which to set the scenario (Figure 3.5). Students needed to consider the development around Iroquois Ridge High School, with its impact on economic, environmental, and social and political issues.

Set in this framework, various questions emerged, such as:

■ What happens to the town's property taxes with development?
■ What is the result of a loss of agriculture?
■ What happens to local jobs?
■ What would happen if the entire world lived this way?

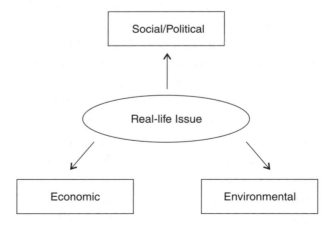

**FIGURE 3.5
Aspects to Consider**

FIGURE 3.6
MILLENNIUM PROJECT RUBRICS
Research/Data Collection

Criteria	Level 1	Level 2	Level 3	Level 4
Planning the Research Process	Identifies the information specific to completing the task/solving the problem with minimal effectiveness Chooses the use of primary and/or secondary sources of information with minimal effectiveness	Identifies the information specific to completing the task/solving the problem with moderate effectiveness Chooses the use of primary and/or secondary sources of information with moderate effectiveness	Chooses the use of primary and/or secondary sources of information with effectiveness Chooses the use of primary (e.g., student developed surveys, interviews) and/or secondary sources (e.g., published resources) of information effectively	Identifies the information specific to completing the task/solving the problem with high effectiveness Chooses the use of primary and/or secondary sources of information with high effectiveness
Selecting Resources	Uses a variety of published sources and human resources with minimal effectiveness to complete the task Rarely selects the most appropriate sources for the task	Uses a variety of published sources and human resources with moderate effectiveness to complete the task Sometimes selects the most appropriate sources for the task	Uses a variety of published sources (online, print catalogues, encyclopedias, books, journals, etc.) and human resources (e.g., librarians, business, community, site visits) effectively to complete the task Frequently selects the most appropriate souces for the task	Uses a variety of published sources and human resources with high effectiveness to complete the task Routinely selects the most appropriate sources for the task
Locating Information	Uses a limited range of information retrieval strategies to locate appropriate and relevant information from the selected resources	Uses a moderate range of information retrieval strategies to locate appropriate and relevant information from the selected resources	Uses an extensive range of information retrieval strategies to locate appropriate and relevant information from the selected resources (e.g., indexes, directories, table of contents, search engine, keyword searches, interviews, questionnaires)	Uses a complete range of information retrieval strategies to locate appropriate and relevant information from the selected resources
Analyzing Information	Rarely interprets information appropriately to support the hypothesis/solution Rarely identifies factors to validate the accuracy of the information	Sometimes interprets information appropriately to support the hypothesis/solution Sometimes identifies factors to validate the accuracy of the information	Frequently interprets information appropriately to support the hypothesis/solution Frequently identifies factors to validate the accuracy of the information (e.g., author, date, credentials)	Routinely interprets information appropriately to support the hypothesis/solution Routinely identifies factors to validate the accuracy of the information
Use of Information	Rarely presents research information appropriately Sources are rarely accurately recorded and documented	Sometimes presents research information appropriately Sources are sometimes accurately recorded and documented	Frequently presents research information appropriately (e.g., charts, diagrams, text) Sources are frequently accurately recorded and documented	Routinely presents research information appropriately Sources are routinely accurately recorded and documented

From this introduction, students were instructed to focus on one aspect of the situation. They were then to identify a problem and begin solving it. Assessment procedures were explained, and students were given a packet of the rubrics outlining the criteria for their products. The rubrics were similar to the generic rubrics created by the consortium (see Figure 3.6 for a sample rubric for research and data collection). Students were given an individual summative assignment. For this task, they were forewarned that they would be asked to analyze the program and their own learning. They did the final presentation on their learning for each other. There were both teacher and peer assessments.

Students got deeply involved in the project. Since class time was limited, they did a lot of work outside class. There was a wide range of responses. Students focused on a variety of aspects of the issue and ended up doing things such as telephoning developers, and getting blueprints and environmental assessments. Some went on a tour of a current work site. Others surveyed neighbors for their opinions.

From the teachers' perspective, the problem they presented the students was a nebulous one. In fact, some students argued that there was not a problem at all since there was more money after the development for the town and the school. What was important was that students completed a thorough analysis of the situation and demonstrated an understanding of the complexity of an issue in the real world.

The teachers found that their roles shifted. After the introductory day and before the final presentations, students worked independently on their problem. The teachers then became facilitators. They didn't give out information because, as Miller reported, "frankly we didn't know." Students had formed their own groups, and the teachers found that they had to direct them on how to work together better. They also found themselves doing errands such as driving students to look up something or to see something.

Other teachers became involved. Communications ranged, for example, from letters to faxes to presentations. PowerPoint and video cameras were used. Students learned these skills from the appropriate teacher. The history teacher was brought in for local history.

What became quickly apparent was that some of the skills the students needed to learn and execute were not explicit in curriculum documents. Students needed to learn such things as telephone etiquette, interview skills, and how to communicate with a wide range of the public, from construction workers to bureaucrats.

In the final analysis, the teachers were highly pleased with student response. The very good students did really well. But in addition, Miller said, "Some of the kids who don't do that well ordinarily, did superbly." Students were given a lot of freedom and responsibility, which most of them embraced. The project was deemed a success.

The Millennium Project: 300 Students, 60 Teachers

This ambitious pilot at Grand River Collegiate Institute, under the Waterloo Region District School Board, Ontario, involved 300 students and 60 teachers. It ran from September to December over nine half-days. A committee of eight volunteer teachers met periodically over two years to plan this venture. Brett Dubrick and Kirby Julian cochaired these sessions. The committee represented most subject areas. They spent the first half-year developing a vision for what the project might look like. During this time, the committee explained the project to the 60 teachers who would be involved in its implementation. Each teacher would act as a mentor, responsible for facilitating a small group through the process. The staff at Grand River was positive and highly motivated, making it an ideal culture in which to implement such a large-scale pilot.

Staff members used the standards-based performance assessment planning as outlined in Step 7 of Figure 3.2 (page 29). All assessment tasks and accompanying rubrics were introduced to students at the beginning of the project. The culminating presentation was delivered to external assessors who were involved in the real-life context of the problem. This project was worth 5 percent of each grade 11 subject area. Students were presented with the following problem:

The Council for the City of Kitchener is accepting proposals to "renew or enhance" the city or its image. As a part of the proposal, the city is prepared to contribute up to $100,000 to the project. Your task is to develop a detailed plan based upon research that must include the following:

■ Identification and inventory of some problems or needs that are currently unsatisfied.
■ A detailed analysis of the problems that your solution will address.
■ Your proposed solution and implementation strategy with a detailed allocation of funds.
■ A presentation of your plan to a committee of external evaluators from the community—representing a city council—who will assess it based on your solution and your ability to defend your proposal.

In drafting their proposals (Figure 3.7), students approached the problem from many levels. For example, one group focused on beautifying downtown, while another worked on bringing the

Ontario Summer Games to Kitchener. In general, students were quite successful—especially those who had chosen something that was both personally relevant and complex in nature.

Assessment tasks included the following:

■ Completion of the Millennium Project proposal.
■ A group work-in-progress book that included summaries of interviews with mentors and others, brainstorming notes, raw data on appropriate display, evidence of collaboration with individual work, evidence of use of technology, and resources.
■ Individual journals.
■ A written report using word processing—with thesis, results, conclusions, and recommendations, including appropriate charts, tables, graphs, maps, drawings, and so forth.
■ An oral presentation or defense.
■ Project reflections—self and peer evaluation rubrics, and a project reflection form.

The groups delivered a 10- to 15-minute final presentation to external assessors—a subcommittee of city council members and representatives from downtown businesses and the Grand River Conservation Authority. The evaluation component caused both anxiety and inspiration. There was great excitement because the final presentations were so well received. Several groups were requested to bring their presentations in camera to the city council. A copy of another group's presentation was requested by another region with the expressed intent of implementing it.

What problems did Grand River Collegiate Institute encounter during this period? Fortunately problems were minimized because the original committee executed a well-thought-out plan that was streamlined and relatively simple. It was also helpful that parents were very supportive of the program.

Many of the typical concerns with a project such as this were eliminated by the non-semestered

FIGURE 3.7
Millennium Project Proposal

Date: _____

Student Names: _____

Teacher Advisor(s): _____

Description of the Problem: (including the variables) _____

_____

_____

_____

> The information required below must be completed in detail as a Project Team task. The Project Team will meet with a teacher advisor to go over this proposal before work begins.

Resources:

People (school staff, community members, others): _____

Electronic (e.g., the Internet, catalogues, microfiche): _____

Print (periodicals, texts, archives, etc.): _____

Data Collection (specify primary and secondary sources, method of collection): _____

Project Team Responsibilities (describe individual and group responsibilities): _____

Teacher Advisor Signature: _____

Date: _____

school schedule, which featured a five-day rotating timetable with five periods a day to accommodate eight subjects. This was a perfect fit for the Millennium Project. It was scheduled so students missed only three hours of any given class. This eliminated most of the teachers' objections that the project was taking too much time from "their subject area." In addition, the mentors would have some time off when students were working on the project; this would compensate for some of the time they devoted to this new responsibility.

The open-endedness of the problem meant that students could go in any direction to solve it. In practice this meant there was not an overload on resources, as had happened in other areas involved in the Millennium Project. For example, at Iroquois Ridge there was a deluge of calls to the city's administrative council, with students all seeking the same information at the same time.

The students were assigned to groups of four, a process done in English class. Students were asked to select four students they would like to work with, recognizing that possibly only one of their choices would be in their group. Teachers then created the groups. The makeup of the groups did not differ greatly, which was considered preferable since the final assessment was for the most part team-based.

The nine half-days of independent learning were spread between late September and early December. During this time, each group had a mentor with whom it met once weekly. All 60 teachers played the role of mentor, offering structure to the students. Mentors kept in touch with what was happening across the school through a newsletter, *The Weekly Mentor Update*, in which the original planning committee addressed the mentors' questions. Mentors were also given an agenda of upcoming tasks for them to execute.

One difficulty was the necessity to focus on assessment while students were working in indeterminate areas. Since problems were open-ended with

no right answer, the students' products were difficult to assess. Students were to be assessed on teamwork, communication, critical thinking, problem solving, and time management. This new way of thinking about what is important for students to learn was an ongoing issue. Brett Dubrick believes, however, that the teachers are well on the way to getting the assessment piece right. The rubrics, for example, are still being refined to ensure that they measure what they are intended to measure.

Finally, there were some logistical problems with assessing the culminating activity. Three teams of outside assessors evaluated groups for three full days. It was difficult to find and assemble the teams and ask them to devote so much time to the process. The evaluation process, however, was a very positive one. For students it was the highlight of the unit; for the community "experts," it was seen as very worthwhile. According to Brett Dubrick, it created "super public relations" between the school and the community.

As previously mentioned, most of the students did well on this project and enjoyed it. Again, as at Iroquois Ridge, it was noted that students learned things that were never written down. They had to be creative to overcome obstacles. For example, students did not find downtown businesses to be forthcoming if they asked questions in the role of student. However, when they presented themselves as ordinary citizens, they were able to elicit the information they wanted.

Some of the students who had previously struggled academically continued to struggle in the Millennium Project. This was alleviated somewhat by the fact that the students could enter the problem solving at many different levels and could work on something of their own choice. A few students did not complete the project, and they received a 0. This was reflected across all their subjects, since it was worth 5 percent of each subject area. (A point of contention with the teachers had been how much value to put on the project). In addition, a few students misused their time during the independent study block and did not complete work in the time allowed. As a result, they found themselves doing a lot of work at the end. However, the vast majority of students handled the time management well. As at Iroquois Ridge, the project was deemed a success, and teachers looked forward to refining it with the things they learned in the pilot.

Learning Through the Arts

Learning Through the Arts was a comprehensive and complex approach to bringing about school transformation. The program was developed at the Royal Conservatory of Music in Toronto and led by Angela Elster. (She can be reached via e-mail at angelae@rcmusic.ca.) The original pilot project in Toronto included nine schools, 4,000 students, and 200 teachers. A national initiative involved six sites, including 20,000 students and up to 900 teachers.

In this innovative program, the arts are not treated as a separate area of learning and appreciation, but are infused directly into the general curriculum in a manner that enhances a child's ability to learn concepts required in many disciplines. At the heart of the program lies the premise that the discipline, cooperation, creativity, and self-esteem developed in the arts are essential life skills.

PROCESS

STAGE ONE
■ Schools commit to a minimum three-year, full-school implementation process.
■ Teachers at each grade level meet to identify a "big" theme that supports their curriculum.
■ Teachers at each grade level identify areas of the curriculum that would benefit from additional creative, holistic teaching strategies.
■ Teachers at each grade determine three art forms that will support the curriculum areas they have identified.

STAGE TWO
■ Appropriate artists are interviewed and successful candidates added to the roster of artist educators.
■ Artists are divided into teams of three each to aid individual schools and individual grades.

STAGE THREE
■ Artist development sessions provide artists with tools in areas such as provincial curriculum, age appropriateness, classroom management, multiple intelligences, learning styles, special needs, lesson planning, holistic education, and models of integration.
■ Artists meet in their respective teams to explore the theme, plan a sequence, research content, and begin to develop strategies for classroom sessions.
■ Individual artists meet with their grade-specific teacher teams and collaboratively develop the classroom units. Here teachers are led through hands-on artistic processes to develop their skill sets. Together objectives and evaluation tools are developed.

STAGE FOUR
■ In the first term (from late September to December) over a four-to-six-week period, the first artist completes three classroom sessions—with a minimum of one week between sessions—with clear instructions for teacher follow-up and extensions between visits.
■ At the conclusion of the allotted three classroom sessions, the artist and teacher debrief.
■ The process is repeated in the second term with the second artist.
■ The process is repeated in the third term with the third artist.
■ A second artist development session held in January offers additional areas to strengthen artists' skill sets.

These four stages are repeated for a minimum of three years with the same artists and teachers partnering whenever possible. Ongoing assessment is integral to this initiative in order that growth is documented among teachers, students, artists, administrators, and the school board, with both quantitative and qualitative measures. Toward the end of the pilot program in Toronto, Learning Through the Arts officials believed that a majority of teachers had begun using the arts extensively in their teaching and that the culture of these schools had been transformed. Initial results of research indicate that the inclusion of arts into the curriculum does indeed seem to engage students, particularly those with linguistic, cultural, emotional, and behavioral challenges.

The Alpha Program: A Multi-age, Fully Integrated Community

The Alpha Team was established in 1972 in Shelburne, Vt. Carol Smith has been involved since 1975. Today Alpha Team consists of 62 students in grades 6, 7, and 8. Students are organized in three multiage groups, each guided by an Alpha teacher. A daily morning meeting outlines the master schedule, after which students designate time for individual work on their own schedules. The program is inspiring to read about and constructivist in its best sense. Detailed examples of early programs of adopting a business (Smith, Mann, & Steadman, 1993) and putting on a circus (Smith, Blaise, Mann, & Myers, 1993) are available.

What perhaps is most unique about this school is that curriculum is planned by both teachers and students. Based on the work of James Beane (1993, 1997), themes are drawn from the students' personal and social concerns. Between 100 and 500 questions are generated at the beginning of each year. The teachers take these questions, then sort and re-sort them to categorize them into themes. Since students are in this program for three years, they are conscious of the need to rotate themes. The themes—really big ideas, such as economy—offer rich opportunities for learning. Generally, five to seven

themes are explored a year. In addition, participants do a musical, and plan and go on a trip each year.

Assessment receives a heavy emphasis in this program. Diagnostic testing is done three times a year in reading, spelling, and computation. All standardized testing is discipline-specific, but Smith reports that students do very well on the tests. Students are also expected to keep a detailed account of their weekly goals and assessment. Each piece of work is evaluated in some way. Often students develop assessment criteria with the teachers. Students keep a portfolio to document their mastery of a particular goal or standard and their growth toward that goal. Portfolios are presented to parents twice a year in a student-led conference.

To provide a deeper understanding of the Alpha Program, its plan for a unit on government is included.

"We the People"— A Theme Study on Government

Alpha Team: Claire Evenson, Cynthia Myers, Carol Smith, John Downes (Student Intern)
64 Students (6-8)
Time Frame: two weeks of curriculum development and theme organization and planning, with four weeks of theme study

SUMMARY

In the opening weeks of school, the Alpha Team worked together to identify the topics for the year's theme studies. Using theme ideas left over from last year's planning and incorporating questions from new students, the team organized interests into four major themes: government, mysteries, social issues, and environment. The government theme took priority for the beginning of the year because of its natural connection to the year's election.

The words from the preamble to the Constitution of the United States became the organizing structure for the strands of the government study. Each prime group took a section of the preamble as its strand "lens." Based on students' questions about the government, theme strands were further divided into smaller study groups to look into the issues of power, rights and responsibilities, and equality.

SMALL GROUP STRANDS

Each prime group used its constitutional "lens" to identify issues related to power, rights, responsibilities, and equality that still face the government as it is called on to fulfill the promises of the Constitution. Nine ballot items resulted from the work, each reflecting a small group's proposal to begin to resolve the critical issue it found most important. Students wrote persuasive essays and created visual displays and oral presentations to draw support for their ballot item.

INDIVIDUAL PROJECTS

Each student identified a critical question of personal interest and explored it through individual research and interviews. Personal projects were created to highlight the results of each student's research. The students' critical questions included: Is capital punishment fair? Which party's welfare plan best reflects the Preamble of the Constitution? What are my rights as a child in the United States of America? How does the makeup of the Supreme Court affect our government, nation, and laws? How did immigrant Poles come to America? How might the world be different if women had equal rights? What is the role of the three branches of government in gun control?

CULMINATING EVENT

An open house at the culmination of this theme study consisted of three parts. One section was organized so visitors could follow the curriculum planning process. Displaying the process was a visual way to put the pieces of theme planning into perspective and helped parents see the powerful

ways in which students learn throughout a theme study, from its first question to its culmination.

Small-group presentations formed the second section of the culminating event. After listening to each group's presentation and reviewing the research supporting each ballot item, visitors were asked to vote on the nine questions put forth by students. A display of individual projects created to answer each student's critical question made up the third section of the open house.

In this section several examples of integrated curriculum have been provided to offer an idea of the wide range of possibilities for application. There are many more excellent examples happening across North America today.

WORKS CITED

Beane, J. (1993). *A middle school curriculum: From rhetoric to reality.* Columbus, OH: National Middle School Association.

Beane, J. (1997). *Curriculum integration: Designing the core of democratic education.* New York: Teachers College Press.

Jacobs, H. H. (Ed.). (1989). *Interdisciplinary curriculum: Design and development.* Alexandria, VA: Association for Supervision and Curriculum Development.

Lauritzen, C., & Jaeger, M. (1997). *Integrating through story: The narrative curriculum.* Albany, NY: Delmar Publishing.

Lauritzen, C., & Jaeger, M. (1998). The transforming power of literature: "An afternoon in the stacks." *The New Advocate, 11*(3), 229–238.

Ontario Ministry of Education (1997). *The Ontario curriculum, Grades 1–8 science.* Toronto: Ministry of Education and Training, Government of Ontario.

Polacco, P. (1992). *Chicken Sunday.* New York: Philomel.

Russell, C., & Burton, J. (2000, Spring). A report on an Ontario secondary school integrated environmental studies program. *Canadian Journal of Environmental Education, 5*, 287–304.

Schmidt, M., & Plue, L. (2000). New world of performance-based assessment. *Orbit, 30*(4), 14–17.

Smith, C., Blaise, B., Mann, L., & Myers, D. (1993). The big Alpha circus. In C. Stevenson & J. Carr (Eds.), *Integrating studies in the middle grades: Dancing through walls* (pp. 100–107). New York: Teachers College Press.

Smith, C., Mann, L., & Steadman, W. (1993). Adopt a business. In C. Stevenson & J. Carr (Eds.), *Integrating studies in the middle grades: Dancing through walls* (pp. 100–107). New York: Teachers College Press.

Stevenson, C., & Carr, J. (1993). *Dancing through walls*. New York: Teachers College Press.

Wiggins, G., & McTighe, J. (1998). *Understanding by design*. Alexandria, VA: Association for Supervision and Curriculum Development.

IV. QUESTIONS AND ANSWERS

1. What is the role of thematic webbing or curriculum mapping?

When teachers were exploring integrated approaches in the early '90s, they often began with thematic webbing or curriculum mapping (see Erickson, 1995, 1998; Fogarty, 1991; Jacobs, 1989; Palmer, 1991). These activities are fun and allow people to see that connections across subject knowledge bases are endless. This is particularly true when a variety of subject areas are represented.

Today, with the emphasis on standards-based curriculum, I do not find teachers using these techniques very often. Rather, they create standards-based webs by making connections across the standards. See Figure 3.3 (page 31) for an example.

However, alternative webbing or mapping strategies can still be useful as an introductory activity. Examples of three types of webbing activities are found in the Conceptual Framework section of Figure 1.1 on page 4.

Thematic webbing begins with the theme, such as justice, as the organizing center written in the middle of a large piece of newsprint. Participants brainstorm for possible connections to the theme. On the newsprint, lines are drawn between the connections and the theme. Content possibilities, rather than activities, should be emphasized. Once this is done, the material can be reorganized into clusters that are appropriate to teach to the age group in question.

Curriculum mapping is a very different process. Participants write down the organizing center in the middle of the newsprint. The organizing center may be a theme, issue, or process skill. Justice may be in the center of this circle, as in the above example. Often a skill such as information management acts as the organizing center. Selected disciplines are placed on the periphery of the newsprint. The brainstorming is for direct connections within each discipline to the organizing center.

A transdisciplinary web is yet another option. In this case the organizing center involves a real-life context. Instead of brainstorming around a discipline, participants can brainstorm around such contexts—for example, economics, technology, or social issues. It is assumed that the disciplines are embedded in the real-life context. However, subject areas are often identified after the initial brainstorming.

2. How does a teacher's specialized knowledge of subject matter factor into integrated curriculum?

Elementary school teachers often perceive themselves as "teachers who teach kids," while high school teachers perceive that they teach disciplines. Teaching "disciplines" can block integration. However, many skilled high school teachers are welcoming a chance to try new things.

Often a specialist will say it is impossible to integrate in his or her subject area. Music and math teachers, for example, may be concerned that students will not attain basic skills in their areas if they are embedded in an integrated program. Yet other teachers in these same areas have no problem with integration—perception and attitude are sometimes what counts. Still there are times when skills are learned in isolation.

In an elementary school, teachers tend to be more comfortable planning integrated curriculum by themselves. In high schools, team planning is often preferable because varying subject areas and expertise are represented. If the team can't find a place for a subject area in a topic of study, it is usually because a representative is not there. Involve a math or science teacher, and he or she will be able to see the connections.

3. How will teachers know enough to teach an integrated program?

It is quite possible that the teacher will not know enough in areas that are not his or her specialty. This phenomenon will also occur when teachers honor the questions that students ask.

In reality, teachers actually know much more than they give themselves credit for. Still, teachers fear not knowing enough in areas where they are not specialists. Grammar, math, and science often inspire these feelings of inadequacy. This is partially resolved by the willingness of teachers to keep learning new things. They take university courses to upgrade and attend professional development programs. Guest experts can be asked to the class, or students can go into the community to find resources. One of the main purposes of interdisciplinary teaming is to pool expertise from different subject areas. Finally, the teacher needs to be able to tell the student that he or she does not know the answer—and that they will search for it together. (This is one place where administrators' modeling is helpful).

4. How do gifted and low-track students fare in schools using integrated curriculum?

Molly Maloy and Camille Barr are two principals of schools that feature integrative curriculum; they strongly believe that their curriculum benefits all students (Powell, 1999). They believe that the curriculum can be successfully differentiated for all students and that this is the best way they learn.

Integration has long been the domain of the gifted student (Clark, 1986). Today, strategies such as problem-based learning are considered "a perfect match for the creative intelligent student" (Felton, 1998, p. 188). A professor of gifted education once told me that only the gifted could make connections and could function in an integrated program. This is simply not true. Lower-level students can

also do well. Their success surprised some of the teachers in the Millennium Project and delighted Sharon DeFrees in her environmental science class (both featured in Section III). It has been true in my own interdisciplinary teaching experiences. Lower-level students' success has a lot to do with a curriculum that they find meaningful and relevant.

5. What role do the arts play in integration efforts?

Unfortunately, the arts often receive short shrift in times of reform. They are considered frill subjects that must give way to math and sciences. Yet the arts have much to offer. Many believe the arts put us in touch with our humanity and are crucial to any curriculum concerned about "being" in the world. Teachers can focus on higher-order thinking skills at the same time as teaching the arts. The problem-solving process, for example, can be learned explicitly as students tackle creating an art piece (Foshay, 1998).

Others argue that the arts can facilitate the development of the intellect. The Royal Conservatory of Music (1994) in Toronto offers some interesting food for thought:

■ Students who pursued more than four years of music and arts scored 34 points higher on SAT verbal scores and 18 points higher on SAT math than students who took these subjects for less than a year.
■ Students who studied the arts performed 30 percent better in academic skills than those not involved.
■ Students who were considered below average in ability showed substantial academic achievement when a comprehensive approach to the arts was used.

The arts offer a natural way to integrate curriculum with other subject areas. The demonstration for the culminating activity often features performance tasks that revolve around the arts. Students show their understanding of the topic with such things as a drama, a mural, a puppet show, a song, or works of art. Teachers of the arts fear that these types of demonstrations will be required but that the skills and basic understandings necessary will not be taught explicitly. In a standards-based approach, they must be taught. The arts standards can be incorporated into an integrated design. Creating a good product through applying arts skills is central to the performance.

6. How long a unit should be planned?

Start small. The optimum way to begin is to plan a small unit and implement it. This then leads to further planning and implementation. A common pitfall is to plan too much, while not eliminating anything from the old curriculum. A two- or three-week unit is enough to begin with. A common difficulty can be deciding what aspects of the previous curriculum to give up. As one teacher commented, "It's not the case of something not being important. It's the case of something else being more important" (Scott, 1999).

As teachers become more comfortable with integrative approaches, they will begin to make connections automatically. This axiom holds true for individual teachers as well as for teams.

7. How can teachers integrate the curriculum and still cover the content?

In theory, teachers are expected to cover the content. In reality, even teachers in a traditional system are rarely able to cover all of the prescribed content. Wiggins and McTighe (1998) offer a system for deciding what is worth knowing. Three circles help establish curriculum priorities. The largest ring identifies what knowledge students

should find worth knowing. This calls for some basic familiarity with the topic in question. The middle ring is where the important knowledge fits. This includes facts, concepts, principles, and process skills. The students must know the things in this area if they are to master the essentials in the unit. The inner ring represents the "enduring understandings" that anchor the unit. These are the big ideas—the things you want students to take away with them long after the unit is over. In their book, *Understanding by Design*, Wiggins and McTighe pursue this idea in detail.

Once teachers begin to focus this way, they come to understand the phrase "less is more." A criticism often levied at interdisciplinary work is that it can be superficial. This can be true, especially if a teacher includes trite activities in order to say a subject has been included. Taking a thoughtful approach such as Wiggins and McTighe offer allows students to explore a topic of interest in great depth.

8. How can teachers integrate and still cover the standards?

When teachers are first confronted with long lists, they tend to be intimidated and retreat from any integrated approaches they might have been practicing. Fortunately many teachers report that once they have become familiar with a standards-based curriculum, they find they can integrate quite easily without sacrificing required content. Barbara Brodhagen, a middle school teacher in Madison, Wisc., notes that the standards are generally not content-specific and require complex performances in order to demonstrate achievement. For her, interdisciplinary work is the only way she can get students to a point where they are able to demonstrate these complex performances.

Again, the rule of integration and separation must be considered. There are times when a subject such as math does not fit naturally. The math standards are often too abstract, and teachers must teach these skills separately.

Brenda Christie, of the Grand Erie District School Board, Ontario, comments that most of her math skills—such as data management and probability—are taught in geography. She notes that this way of thinking was a lot of work at first, but once she got started it got easier. Now she is working on educating her students to start thinking of achieving the standards first, and second to understand how these standards can be taught through many different lenses or subject areas. This way she hopes to help them make connections and value skills across the curriculum.

Carol Smith, of the Alpha Program, offers a similar solution. The fully integrated program is based on student questions revolving around personal and social concerns. Basically all the general standards are covered. There are times, however, when students don't ask questions about some of the things that are mandated in the standards. Knowing about forces of motion, for example, is not one of the students' questions. To cover these standards, students go to seminars. The seminars tend to be more teacher-directed and often planned for the time between Thanksgiving and Christmas. They last for two hours each day for about a week; the students enjoy this variety in instructional techniques.

9. How can teachers make sense of the various approaches to standards?

In an interesting article called "Standards Are My Friends" (2000), teacher Mary Jo Zeigler describes how she used standards to develop an integrated project for 6th grade. As she became familiar with the district standards, she found them filled with skills and ideas that she thought were important to learn. However, she found their presentation very confusing. Some did not differentiate by grade

levels; some used benchmarks, others used criteria; and all were pages and pages long and intimidating. She then separated out the core standards in each subject area and pared that down to one page per subject area. Each page was very crowded with standards and benchmarks and left no room for notes or documenting. She reorganized all the standards and benchmarks for which she was responsible. This time she left lots of room to list the unit and the activities in which the standard was addressed. She was left with documents that were fairly easy to use and not intimidating.

10. How do teachers prepare students for standardized tests?

Standardized tests are a current reality and can't be avoided. Integrated curriculum tends to best be measured by performance assessment, rubrics, portfolios, self-assessment, and peer assessment. Teachers may, however, take some comfort in knowing that research suggests that students who are taught through an interdisciplinary approach will do at least as well on standardized and other measures as students who learned through the disciplines (Vars, 1996, 2000).

Teachers also informally report that since they have focused on higher-order thinking skills in integrated approaches, students can think their way through standardized tests. The students in the fully integrated Alpha Program in Vermont, for example, do very well on standardized tests—and this is a heterogeneous population with a wide range of student abilities.

Glatthorn (1999) offers a creative way in which teachers can align the curriculum with standardized tests and still create in-depth units of study that will likely engage students. In some ways, it is similar to Wiggins and McTighe's (1998) approach offered above, but it is geared to testing. First, you analyze the school district's written curriculum in terms of mastery, organic, and enrichment categories. Mastery curriculum is essential for all students to learn, is based on standards, is geared to one grade level, and is likely to be tested. Organic curriculum is essential for students to learn, is found throughout the grade levels, and is usually not tested. Enrichment curriculum is nice for students to learn. Teachers then review their identification of mastery benchmarks by checking the curriculum, nonconfidential information about the tests available through state department practice tests, and the textbooks. By clustering related mastery benchmarks and using their own creativity, Glatthorn suggests teachers are in a position to create interesting curriculum while still preparing students to do well on high-stakes testing.

Glatthorn offers the following example. A mastery benchmark is: "Understands the similarities and differences in Colonial concepts of community." The benchmark for the organic curriculum is: "Knows how to perceive past events with historical empathy." The enrichment benchmark would be: "Understands differences among several states' constitutions." These can be the foundation for a unit called "Whose community?" which can begin with students' understanding of their community, examining the concept of an ideal community and emphasizing some of the similarities and differences among the Colonial communities. Glatthorn believes that this would be relevant to the students.

11. How can we report achievement on integrated subjects on traditional report cards?

Integration works best when the reporting, assessment, and standards are aligned in a way that support its basic premises. However, there are not many districts where this is a reality. Traditionally, grades for subject areas are recorded. Process skills such as communication are often recognized on the report card, but they are not as highly valued as the marks for disciplines. In reality, what is assessed or reported is what becomes important to learn.

How do teachers deal with the reality of the traditional report card? Bob Ogilvie, of Grand Erie District School Board in Ontario, stresses that reporting from an integrated lens involves learning how to assess holistically. It begins by connecting standards to assessment when creating performance assessment tasks. Mike McDonald, also at Grand Erie, advises teachers to assess how well the student achieved the standards within the assignment, rather than assessing the assignment itself.

Yet teachers who teach in an integrated fashion often need to justify where the "geography" mark on the report card came from. One solution is to give the same grade for each subject involved, as in the Millennium Project. With some experience, teachers find they can differentiate subjects within the activities in which students participate.

12. How do we change reporting, assessment, and standards to align with an integrated approach?

In part, changing traditional reporting requires reeducating many of us—parents and educators alike. Parents want a report card that allows them to understand how their child is doing. They understand what a grade in a subject area means based on their own experiences in schools.

This is really an opportunity for teachers to introduce parents and guardians to standards-based performance assessment and portfolios. A most powerful tool to convince parents is student-led conferencing (Harris & Carr, 1996). Students review their work in the context of standards, criteria and performance indicators. The teacher is there to supplement the child's view and add his or her perspective. Harris and Carr warn that it is crucial that students have had an opportunity to truly understand the standards and can explain them in their own words.

Educators and parents need to question what is worth knowing and therefore worth reporting. As territorial battles over subject areas are reconciled, it seems that the standards that connect disciplines will emerge as essential to know and therefore to assess. For the time being, we can support the learning of cross-disciplinary standards with our students and to our parents in our individual contexts.

13. How does integrated curriculum fit into long-term planning?

Long-term planning means planning for the year ahead. Rosemary Hunter, of Brock University, offers the following process for long-range planning. She advises using a wide-angle lens first to see the whole picture and then a zoom lens to see each subject, each month, each unit, and each lesson. It is key that the standards are aligned with the assessment and instructional strategies. Questions to start aligning curriculum should be:

■ What do the students need to know, be able to do, and be like?
■ How can I recognize what they know, can do, and are like?
■ How can I teach this concept, skill, or value?
■ How will the students learn best?

Hunter emphasizes two essential tasks: separation and integration, in parallel with simplifying and connecting. Teachers need to discern what is best taught alone as an isolated concept or skill and when it makes more sense to connect things in a context or through a central focus or theme.

She offers the following process for long-range planning:

■ View all subject standards.
■ Work with one subject at a time.

■ Look at the most general standards for strands and topics within a subject.
■ Group content and skills from general standards on the basis of commonalities.
■ Match specific standards that support general ones.
■ Align assessment and instruction.
■ Repeat the process for all subjects.
■ Organize curriculum groupings by the month.
■ Look for connections for integration.
■ Choose themes for a month.
■ Identify stand-alone content.

14. How can a repetition of the same themes and concepts year after year be avoided?

At the school level, curriculum mapping is an important first step in the integration process. In *Mapping the Big Picture*, Jacobs (1997) outlines a process for using the school calendar to plan instruction. Teachers map horizontally across one grade level to see what topics are being studied. As well, curriculum is mapped vertically through all grade levels. In this way teachers can see where subjects come together and where they might plan for interdisciplinary work.

Rebecca Burns, of the Appalachia Educational Laboratory, offers a more sophisticated version that she calls a Teaching/Learning Mapping Strategy (TLMS). This is an electronic mapping and design tool that helps teachers and administrators develop a picture of teaching and learning across a district or school. Each teacher or teaching team defines or maps a year's curriculum in monthly "chunks." The completed map shows at a glance what is being taught, when and how it is taught, how it is assessed, and what standards are addressed in every classroom. The maps also include cross-disciplinary connections and potential areas for curriculum integration.

Once the TLMS has been used and a picture is completed, it reveals areas that need improvement in order for students to achieve higher standards. The intent is to align curriculum, instruction, and assessment so that they are coherent and consistent with standards. In two school districts that have used TLMS for one year, student scores on standardized tests improved considerably. One of these Virginia districts now leads the state in percentage point gains in five of 16 core areas that were tested; it ranked in the top 10 in six other areas. Teachers who use TLMS also report increased student engagement in the classroom and higher-order thinking. More information is available at 1-800-624-9120 or by e-mailing Burns at burnsr@ael.org.

15. How can school administrators support teachers who try integrated curriculum?

The support of the administrative leader is a most important part of the process. Most teachers appreciate a nondirective leader.

To meet the challenge of creating integrated curriculum, Kain (1993) suggests that administrators

■ Carefully select team members.
■ Take an active role in monitoring team growth.
■ Plan for workshops.
■ Plan site visits to locations where similar programs are being implemented.
■ Provide release time.

Developing integrated curriculum involves change. Once interdisciplinary curriculum is implemented, both philosophies and practices tend to change radically. The change process is challenging even when the change is embraced. It is a process, not an event. Schools who moved to fully integrated approaches reported that it occurred over a three- to five-year time frame (Van Zandt & Albright, 1996).

For the individuals involved, change involves stages of emotional responses (Drake, 1993). It

begins with resistance and grief (letting go of the old), and moves on through conflict and struggle (confronting the obstacles of new practices) to joy (when the new practices become institutionalized). Administrators will personally experience these stages; they will also need to support the staff through this long and often painful process.

When the school has a collaborative culture, real change is possible (Hargreaves, 1994). The most successful schools have teachers and administrators who form a professional learning community, are focused on student success through assessment, and change their practices according to the assessment results (Newman & Wehlage, 1995).

Fullan (2000) reminds us that change must come from the top down and bottom up. Schools must be connected to the outside community, not just to their own core development. Fullan urges administrators to both restructure (change the structures and roles in a formal organization) and reculture (develop a professional learning community).

Mae Denby, who held central office responsibilities for curriculum under a midsize school board, suggests that certain fundamental questions should be addressed as a part of the reculturing effort:

■ Does the culture support change?
■ Are administrators seen as fully committed to growth and learning?
■ Does the system make support available for innovative ventures?
■ Are the core beliefs among the staff compatible?
■ Are there time and opportunities for teacher talk?
■ Do teachers have opportunities for collaboration?
■ Is ongoing professional development a part of the culture?
■ Do experts from the outside periodically share their expertise?
■ Are teachers encouraged to take risks?
■ Are teachers encouraged to learn from their mistakes?

■ Are student results the focus of school efforts?
■ Are assessment practices and results taken seriously?

Burns (1995) outlines additional factors she believes are essential to successful curriculum integration:

■ Dissolving departmental boundaries to create new work areas and teams
■ "Less is more" as a principle of planning
■ Teacher as facilitator
■ Opportunities for students to learn in the community
■ Classroom culture that is active, collaborative, and self-directed
■ Teachers' beliefs that all students can learn
■ Staff dissatisfaction with the status quo
■ A perception of the advantages of integrated curriculum
■ Teachers as team players
■ Ongoing professional development
■ Action research done by teachers

Administrators can contribute greatly to the success of change efforts around integrated curriculum if they are seen as a model. Dorothy Fowler, an elementary principal under the Halton District School Board, Ontario, consciously sets out to create a culture for her school in which integrated approaches are the norm. She goes out of her way to provide professional development opportunities for her staff and time to plan curriculum. She is willing to go out on a limb and is constantly stretching herself to learn new things. It is hardly surprising that there continue to be wonderful integrated efforts in her school.

Jackie DeLong is another model of a lifelong learner. Today she occupies the role of supervisory officer for the Grand Erie District School Board, Ontario. She has set up a network of teachers who

practice action research. She organizes a yearly provincial conference for teachers to share their research and is coeditor of the electronic journal *Ontario Action Researcher*, available at http://www.unipissing.ca/oar/index.htm. She is also involved in teaching a master of education cohort program at Brock University that focuses on action research. It is striking to witness the excitement at this board and how many of the action research projects revolve around constructivism and integrated approaches.

16. How can we find time to integrate the curriculum?

Time to plan is a key ingredient to success. Yet teachers seem to be getting less time for such activities and have more expectations placed upon them. The following are successful ways that administrators have found time:

■ Implement block scheduling.
■ Schedule similar breaks and preparation times for teachers who are working together.
■ Provide one or two full days for initial curriculum planning if possible, followed by regular half-days.
■ Plan for districtwide professional development days when teachers are encouraged to share curriculum units.
■ Make district seed money available for school projects so that classes can be covered while teachers plan. This has proven to be a very successful tactic.
■ Open an hour later one day a week.
■ Schedule students for independent study for a time slot each week.
■ Provide a pizza dinner for a teacher meeting.
■ Encourage teachers voluntarily to come to school 15 minutes early on Monday and delay the start of classes by 15 minutes. In addition, reduce each class period by five minutes. This allows for 45 minutes of

collaborative time plus 15 minutes extra before school (Mann, 2000).

■ Once a week, have grade 2 classes meet with grade 5, for example, in a buddy system. The next week the teachers reverse who has time off (Mann, 2000).

■ Trade and rearrange time in four-by-four blocks so teachers can take advantage of daylong planning sessions. In the most popular version of this plan, students go to regular class for four days a week and attend a daylong class on Wednesday (Mann, 2000).

17. Who should work on integrated teams?

Working collaboratively is very difficult at the best of times. Projects can be easily sabotaged. Volunteers work best in the initial stages (Van Zandt & Albright, 1996). The team should consist of the people who will be implementing the curriculum. Sometimes a lot of people are included for political reasons but are actually peripheral to the implementation, and this often leads to problems. Do consider including the teacher librarian, curriculum consultant, special education teacher, and technology consultant.

Occasionally an administrator is on the actual implementation team. This can work well if he or she is knowledgeable in curriculum processes and can attend the meetings regularly. In other cases, however, the administrator has either assigned a team leader or lets one emerge. Both strategies have advantages and disadvantages. Working with the concept of an emerging leader can be chaotic, and different people will probably come to the forefront at different times during the process. An assigned leader, however, needs to have good facilitation skills and established credibility before entering this arrangement. In addition, he or she needs to be able to turn over parts of the process when expertise emerges from team members.

Often there are only one or two integrated

teams in a school. A common pitfall of this can be that these teams may be resented by the rest of the school staff, who perceive that they are being treated as favorites. The administrator can guard against this by equalizing resources for all teachers and by offering opportunities for others to establish teams.

How many people should be on a team? Any group of more than seven will be unwieldy. Bishop and Stevenson (2000) believe that teams of four members find it difficult to truly integrate. They recommend two-to-three-person "partner teams" who work together to develop a comprehensive, coherent educational program for approximately 40 to 75 students.

18. What can teachers expect if they join an integrated planning team?

Integrated teams that begin well have fewer difficulties throughout the process than those who experience problems from the start (Kain, 1993). Still, it is a challenging process. Conflict, however, is an essential part of the collaborative process. Support needs to be provided through the following four stages of team growth (Tuckman, as cited in Maurer, 1994):

1. Forming stage—rules and roles are decided and people get to know each other.
2. Storming stage—members become defensive and territorial and block the process of integration.
3. Norming stage—the team finds its rhythm and begins to work together seriously.
4. Performing stage—the team enters the productive stage in which the product is created.

Our research in Ontario consistently showed that working on an interdisciplinary team was a satisfying experience. Teachers reported that working on collaborative teams was both the most exhausting and exciting time of their careers. As teachers began to teach with an integrated perspective and made connections naturally, the exhaustion was eliminated and they were energized.

19. What can educators do to educate and inform parents and community members about their integrated curriculum efforts?

Integrated programs should be shared with parents or guardians. In some schools, parents are a part of the planning process. Carol Smith notes that the desire among parents in her community for an enriched program for students was the catalyst for the fully integrated Alpha program. At a new high school, an advisory council that included community members helped plan the direction of the school's integrated programs. Any public concerns were sent to the council rather than administrators or teachers. Since the council was a part of planning the process, it defended the innovations.

Parents can be sent home with extensive plans to educate them on special projects that their children will be involved in. I was astonished by the number of parents who informally reported to me, with some degree of excitement, about an integrated project in which their children had taken part. They had received information from the school and had listened to the children as they experienced the program. This was a powerful combination. The information allowed parents to talk knowledgeably with their children about what was happening at school. Also, it acquainted parents with the philosophy embedded in most integrated projects. And parents had the opportunity to act as knowledge resources or to help out in chaperon roles. Finally, the enthusiasm and involvement of their children often won them over to interdisciplinary projects.

20. What is the future of integrated curriculum?

In a world with increasingly sophisticated new technology, knowledge is increasing at a dramatic rate. A new set of skills is necessary to successfully compete in the global market. Educators must address this new context. Now, as never before, it is important that school be relevant.

In addition, we live in times when violence and social issues are of special concern to schools. The traditional definition of family is being challenged, and schools appear to be called upon to play a large part in students' moral development.

Yet it has become apparent that none of these concerns can be addressed in a traditional discipline-based system that focuses on academic facts. The old solutions no longer work. It is not possible to sort information into neat boxes, although the traditions and procedures of the disciplines still offer useful ways to examine problems. Problem solving is usually more powerful when approached through the multiple lenses of a variety of disciplines.

The reality is that education is fundamentally changing. What is worth knowing is shifting, from facts to concepts and skills. Innovative instructional strategies are being employed as we know more about how people learn. We are beginning to understand how to assess and evaluate in ways that connect to what is worth knowing. Integrated curriculum is a powerful way to approach these fundamental changes. It seems inevitable, then, that an interdisciplinary focus will be a dominant force in the future—much as disciplines were in the 20th century.

WORKS CITED

Bishop, P., & Stevenson, C. (2000). When smaller is greater: Two or three person partner teams. *Middle School Journal, 3*(3), 12.

Burns, R. C. (1995). *Dissolving the boundaries; Planning for curriculum integration in middle and secondary school.* Charleston, WV: Appalachia Educational Laboratory.

Clark, B. (1986). *Optimizing learning: The integrative education model in the classroom.* Columbus, OH: Merrill.

Drake, S. (1993). *Planning integrated curriculum: The call to adventure.* Alexandria, VA: Association for Supervision and Curriculum Development.

Erickson, H. L. (1995). *Stirring the head, heart and soul: Redefining curriculum and instruction.* Thousand Oaks, CA: Corwin.

Erickson, H. L. (1998). *Concept-based curriculum and instruction: Teaching beyond the facts.* Thousand Oaks, CA: Corwin.

Felton, T. A. (1998). The "ill-structured problem" is NO PROBLEM for gifted curriculum design. *Gifted Education International, 12*(3), 188–189.

Fogarty, R. (1991). *The mindful school: How to integrate the curricula.* Palatine, IL: SkyLight.

Foshay, A. W. W. (1998). Problem solving and the arts. *Journal of Curriculum and Supervision, 13*(4), 328–338.

Fullan, M. (2000). The three stories of educational reform. *Phi Delta Kappan, 81*(8), 581–584.

Glatthorn, A. A. (1999). Curriculum alignment revisited. *Journal of Curriculum and Supervision, 13*(1), 26–34.

Hargreaves, A. (1994). *Changing teachers, changing times.* Toronto: OISE Press.

Harris, D. E., & Carr, J. F. (1996). *How to use standards in the classroom.* Alexandria, VA: Association for Supervision and Curriculum Development.

Jacobs, H. H. (Ed.). (1989). *Interdisciplinary curriculum: Design and development.* Alexandria, VA: Association for Supervision and Curriculum Development.

Jacobs, H. H. (1997). *Mapping the big picture: Integrating curriculum and assessment K–12.* Alexandria, VA: Association for Supervision and Curriculum Development.

Kain, D. L. (1993). Deciding to integrate the curricula: Judgments about holding and stretching. *Research in Middle Level Education, 16*(2), 25–42.

Mann, L. (2000, May). Finding time to collaborate. *Education Update, 43*(2), 1, 3, 8.

Maurer, R. E. (1994). *Designing interdisciplinary curriculum in middle, junior high, and high schools.* Needham Heights, MA: Allyn & Bacon.

Newman, F., & Wehlage, G. (1995). *Successful school restructuring.* Madison, WI: Center on Organization and Restructuring of Schools, University of Wisconsin.

Palmer, J. (1991). Planning wheels turn curriculum around. *Educational Leadership, 49*(2), 57–60.

Powell, R. R. (1999). Reflections on integrative curriculum: A conversation with Camille Barr and Molly Maloy. *Middle School Journal, 31*(2), 25–34.

Royal Conservatory of Music. (1994). *Community arts and education partnership: Towards a comprehensive arts and education program for Metropolitan Toronto through community partnerships. Assessment and recommendations.* Toronto, Ontario: Author.

Scott, R. (1999, December). *Integrated curriculum model in a middle school.* Paper presented at the Ontario Educational Research Conference, Toronto, Ontario.

Van Zandt, L. M., & Albright, S. (1996). The implementation of interdisciplinary curriculum and instruction. In P. S. Hlebowitch & W. W. Wraga (Eds.), *Annual review of research for school leaders* (pp. 166–201). New York: Scholastic.

Vars, G. F. (1996). Effects of interdisciplinary curriculum and instruction. In P. Hlebowitch & W. Wraga (Eds.), *Annual review of research for school leaders* (pp. 148–164). New York: Scholastic.

Vars, G. (2000). Editorial comment: On research, high-stakes testing, and core philosophy. *The Core Teacher, 50*(3), 1.

Wiggins, G., & McTighe, J. (1998). *Understanding by design.* Alexandria, VA: Association for Supervision and Curriculum Development.

Zeigler, M. J. (2000). Standards are our friends. *The Core Teacher, 50*(1), 4–6.

V. CURRICULUM RESOURCES

The resources offered here are ones that people in the field have found useful. This list is not intended to be inclusive.

ANNOTATED BIBLIOGRAPHY

Drake, S. M. (1998). *Creating integrated curriculum: Proven ways to increase student learning.* **Thousand Oaks, CA: Corwin Press.**
This book offers applications for several well-known curriculum designs including those of Heidi Jacobs, Lynne Erickson, Robin Fogarty, Roger Taylor, James Beane, and Carol Lauritzen and Michael Jaeger. It also explores teaching, learning, and assessment from the multidisciplinary, interdisciplinary, and transdisciplinary points of view.

Beane, J. (1993). *A middle school curriculum: From rhetoric to reality.* **Columbus, OH: National Middle School Association.**
Beane, J. (1997). *Curriculum integration: Designing the core of democratic education.* **New York: Teachers College Press.**
Both of these books outline Beane's philosophy of education. The earliest one offers explicit instructions on the "how to." This is a very popular model that has been adapted successfully by many schools, particularly at the middle school level.

Burns, R. (1995). *Dissolving the boundaries: Planning for curriculum integration in middle and secondary school.* **Charleston, WV: Appalachia Educational Laboratory.**
This is a useful primer for those who wish to facilitate interdisciplinary teaming in their schools. Educators can obtain more information on Appalachia Educational Laboratory's Web page (http://www.ael.org), by telephone, (800-624-9120), or through an e-mail list server on interdisciplinary teamed instruction (iti@ael.org).

Erickson H. L. (1995). *Stirring the head, heart, and soul.* **Thousand Oaks, CA: Corwin Press.**
Erickson, H. L. (1998). *Concept-based curriculum and instruction: Teaching beyond the facts.* **Thousand Oaks, CA: Corwin Press.**
Both of these books do an excellent job of outlining in detail how to build concept-based curriculum. They are very useful for educators who want to get a solid grasp on what is worth knowing and how to incorporate that into curriculum design.

Fleming, D. S. (in press). *A teacher's guide to project-based learning.* **Charleston, WV: Appalachia Educational Laboratory.**
This book offers descriptions of projects from across the United States. It gives contact information, a description of the project, learning goals and standards, activities, and assessment. It is a very useful resource with a wide range of ideas. Educators can obtain more information on Appalachia Educational Laboratory's Web page (http://www. ael.org) or by telephone (800-624-9120).

Hlebowitsh, P. S., & Wraga, W. (Eds.). (1996). *Annual review of research for school leaders.* **New York: Scholastic.**
This book has three important chapters that review the history of integration, the success of such programs, and the implementation processes. The book is available from the National Association for Core Curriculum (e-mail: GVarsNACC@aol.com).

Lauritzen, C., & Jaeger, M. (1997). *Integrating through story: The narrative curriculum.* **Albany, NY: Delmar.**
This is an interesting book written by a language arts and a science educator. The curriculum is integrated through the use of fiction and student questioning. A sample of the authors' thinking is

available on the Web page, Thinking Like Great Inventors, at http://redtail.eou.edu/sebp/Inventors/home.html.

Stevenson, C., & Carr, J. F. (Eds.). (1993). *Integrated studies in the middle school: Dancing through walls*. New York: Teachers College Press. This book offers an integrated planning framework and 13 comprehensive stories of successful curriculum integration. It is great for new ideas and possibilities but was written before the emphasis on standards.

NEWSLETTERS

The Core Teacher
National Association for Core Curriculum
110 East Summit Street, Suite 5
Kent, OH 44240-4094
E-mail: GvarsNACC@aol.com
Membership includes the quarterly newsletter ($10.00), edited by Gordon Vars. This excellent newsletter describes the latest developments in interdisciplinary curriculum and core curriculum.

RECOMMENDED JOURNALS

Middle School Journal
Science Teacher
These two journals usually include at least one article that involves interdisciplinary curriculum.

VI. ASCD RESOURCES

The following list is a sampling of the many ASCD resources available on integrated curriculum. For more information about these and other ASCD products and services, contact the ASCD Service Center at 800-933-2723 or 703-578-9600. Or visit ASCD's Online Store at http://www.ascd.org.

BOOKS

Interdisciplinary Curriculum: Design and Implementation
Heidi Hayes Jacobs, Ed.

Presents six design options for an interdisciplinary curriculum and a process for integrating the teaching of science, math, language arts, social studies, and the arts—plus two successful case studies of interdisciplinary programs. 1989. 97 pages.

> Product #611-89156-L41
> Price: $13.95 ASCD members
> $16.95 nonmembers

Planning Integrated Curriculum: The Call to Adventure
Susan M. Drake

Tells how teams work collaboratively to create integrated curricula. 1993. 58 pages.

> Product #611-93025-L41
> Price: $8.95 ASCD members
> $10.95 nonmembers

Teaching Middle School Students to Be Active Researchers
Judith M. Zorfass with Harriet Copel

This book offers middle school educators practical information about inquiry-based, interdisciplinary learning. The authors explore

■ The underlying cognitive, social, and moral reasons why it is developmentally appropriate for young adolescents to become active researchers.

■ How the I-Search—one kind of inquiry-based interdisciplinary unit—translates theory into practice in a manageable way so that it fits into the real lives of middle school teachers.

■ What teaching, learning, and assessment within an I-Search Unit look like in practice and how this relates to technology use, content-area standards, and current theories of education.

■ How to promote successful implementation by having facilitators and administrators create the supportive structures teachers need to engage in cycles of curriculum design, implementation, and evaluation.

Based on 10 years' work with middle schools and interdisciplinary teams, this book shows teachers and students asking real-life questions, searching for answers, and presenting their new understanding of "overarching concepts"—from the effect of overfishing on a region's economy, to the social and emotional effects of natural disasters, to the health implications of water pollution. Teachers and students explored community resources, read varied materials, conducted interviews, and used technology to keep track of their work, which culminated in I-Search reports and exhibits. 1999. 120 pages.

> Product #198180-L41
> Price: $15.95 ASCD members
> $18.95 nonmembers

VIDEOTAPES

Planning Integrated Units: A Concept-Based Approach

Now you can take teachers through every step in the curriculum integration process with this powerful resource. Videoclips follow a team of 4th grade teachers as they plan integrated units based on concepts that relate to students' lives. While observing this firsthand experience, teachers learn how to teach for deeper understanding of content; how to plan units and lessons that help students transfer what they've learned from one subject to the next; how to create integrated units with a concept-based approach; and how to make learning more exciting and fun.

Includes one 65-minute videotape and a facilitator's guide.

Product #497192-L41
Price: $328 ASCD members
$398 nonmembers

Integrating the Curriculum
Heidi Hayes Jacobs

This two-tape series focuses on curriculum integration in elementary, middle, and high schools. Includes a facilitator's guide and the ASCD book, *Interdisciplinary Curriculum: Design and Implementation.*

Product #614248-L41
Price: $490 ASCD members
$590 nonmembers

What's New in School: A Parent's Guide to Curriculum Integration

Aimed at a parent audience, this video explains the basic principles of curriculum integration and how it helps students see connections in what they're learning, including traditional skills. Includes handouts and suggestions for using the video in PTA, school board, and other community meetings.

Product #494181-L41
Price: $65 ASCD members
$95 nonmembers

AUDIOTAPES
Implementing a Relevant, Interdisciplinary Curriculum Utilizing Problem-Based Learning Strategies
Susan M. Butler

Demonstrates the problem-based learning model as participants brainstorm and address issues

surrounding the implementation of problem-based learning in the classroom. Sample design templates and critiquing guides are used to assess the quality of a sample problem. Participants submit a problem-based learning lesson plan to the "Interdisciplinary Problems" Web page maintained by North Carolina State University. Recorded at the 2000 ASCD Annual Conference and Exhibit Show.

Product #200119-L41
Price: $11.95 ASCD members
$14.95 nonmembers

The Design and Implementation of Interdisciplinary Curriculums

(A set of seven audiotapes in a binder)
1. *Designing Interdisciplinary Curriculum K–12* by Heidi Hayes Jacobs
2. *Developing Interdisciplinary Outcome-Based Frameworks* by Kathleen Fitzpatrick
3. *Interdisciplinary Curriculum and Alternative Forms of Assessment* by Bena Kallick
4. *Curriculum Integration, Whole Language, and Teacher Action Research in an Urban Elementary School* by Sharon Denero and Sherrie Gibney-Sherman
5. *Curriculum Integration in Urban Middle Schools* by Laverne Flowers
6. *Integrating Curriculum and Performance at the High School Level* by Jane Pollock
7. *Keeping Content Alive: What Is the Relationship Between Integrating the Curriculum and the New Discipline-Based Content Standards?* by Frank Betts

Product #612-92164-L41
Price: $54.00 ASCD members
$67.50 nonmembers

On Curriculum Integration
Heidi Hayes Jacobs

Reviews six types of curriculum integration, explaining why it improves curriculum and increases motivation. Numerous tips for beginning the curriculum integration process, and how to plan a yearlong integrated curriculum. 1995. 50 minutes.

> Product #295189-L41
>
> Price: $14.95 ASCD members
>
> $17.95 nonmembers

Designing Integrated Curriculum: A Conceptual Framework
Heidi Hayes Jacobs

Outlines a four-step process to create integrated curriculum for performance-based outcomes.

> Product #295027-L41
>
> Price: $9.95 ASCD members
>
> $11.95 nonmembers

Designing Integrated Curriculum That Promotes Higher-Level Thinking
Lynn Erickson

Explores how to design concept-based, integrated teaching units that involve students in cooperative, hands-on learning. 1996. Six hours on four cassettes.

> Product #296202-L41
>
> Price: $29 ASCD members
>
> $35 nonmembers

Connecting the Curriculum: Using an Integrated Interdisciplinary, Thematic Approach
T. Roger Taylor

Participants will learn about interdisciplinary models that emphasize literature-based strategies, higher-order thinking skills, multiple intelligences, cooperative learning, the essential elements of effective instruction, performance-based assessment, brain-based teaching and learning styles, and affective-based teaching.

> Product #297093-L41
>
> Price: $11.95 ASCD members
>
> $14.95 nonmembers

Teachers as Decision Makers: Designing Integrated Curriculum
Ruth Loring

This live recording from the 1999 ASCD Annual Conference explains ways to design integrated curriculum by interlocking academic and technical content with thinking skills and processes. Describes the use of active learning principles and techniques within the context of experiential, situated learning anchored in real-world applications. Focuses on the skillful thinking required in both process and product development. Enhances the development of instructional leadership. Discusses the design process and implications for student achievement, engagement, and motivation.

> Product #299196-L41
>
> Price: $11.95 ASCD members
>
> $14.95 nonmembers

Concept-Based, Integrated Curriculum
Lynn Erickson

Shares perspectives, tips, and examples for creating higher level integration, integrated thinking, and addresses critical questions.

> Product #298112-L41
>
> Price: $11.95 ASCD members
>
> $14.95 nonmembers

Integrated and Authentic Curriculum Development
Robert Hanson

A national authority on curriculum development presents an integrated approach through the use of the five Ps of design.

> Product #298135-L41
>
> Price: $11.95 ASCD members
>
> $14.95 nonmembers

PROFESSIONAL INQUIRY KIT
Curriculum Integration
Carol Cummings

Professional Inquiry Kits provide teachers with a creative and relatively inexpensive tool for staff development. Use of this kit in smaller groups offers participants the opportunity to learn and apply new ideas on curriculum integration. There are eight folders. Folder 1 provides teachers with a rationale and clear instructions on forming a successful study group. The remaining folders focus on the following: Folder 2: Rationale for Curriculum Integration; Folder 3: The Curriculum Map, Web, and Guiding Questions; Folder 4: Extending Integration to Applied Learning and Emotional Intelligence; Folder 5: Designing Authentic Tasks; Folder 6: Active Involvement—Learning Centers and Menus; Folder 7: Putting It All Together; Folder 8: Extending Your Learning. In addition to the eight folders, this kit includes a videotape of clips that support the activities presented.

Product #998214-L41
Price: $159 ASCD members
           $191 nonmembers

ASCD NETWORK
Interdisciplinary Curriculum and Instruction

Through ASCD networks, educators with a common interest exchange ideas and share resources. Networks offer benefits such as newsletters, member directories, bibliographies, clearinghouses, or regional conferences. Some networks charge a nominal fee for their services.

For more information about this network, or to join, contact the network facilitator:

Lois A. Stanciak, Associate Principal
Shepard High School
13049 S. Ridgeland Ave.
Palos Heights, IL 60463 USA
Phone: 708-371-1111, ext. 106
Fax: 708-371-8392
E-Mail: stancial@d218.k12.il.us

SELECTED ARTICLES FROM ASCD PUBLICATIONS

The articles reprinted in the following pages address issues related to this Curriculum Handbook *chapter on integrated curriculum. They are included to help curriculum planners better understand the issues and practices related to integrated curriculum; they are not intended, however, to express ASCD's position on the topics in question.*

"Designing Effective Interdisciplinary Anchors"
By Sasha A. Barab and Anita Landa
Educational Leadership
March 1997, Vol. 54, No. 6, pp. 52–55.

"Teaching for Understanding—Within and Across the Disciplines"
By Howard Gardner and Veronica Boix-Mansilla
Educational Leadership
February 1994, Vol. 51, No. 5, pp. 14–18.

"Courting Controversy: How to Build Interdisciplinary Units"
By Jackie Williams and Terry Deal Reynolds
Educational Leadership
April 1993, Vol. 50, No. 7, pp. 13–15.

"Planning for Curriculum Integration"
By Heidi Hayes Jacobs
Educational Leadership
October 1991, Vol. 49, No. 2, pp. 27–28.

"A Caveat: Curriculum Integration Isn't Always a Good Idea"
By Jere Brophy and Janet Alleman
Educational Leadership
October 1991, Vol. 49, No. 2, p. 66.

"Refocusing the Curriculum: Making Interdisciplinary Efforts Work"
By Scott Willis
Education Update
January 1995, Vol. 37, No. 1, pp. 1, 3, 8.

"Teaching Across Disciplines: Interest Remains High Despite Concerns Over Coverage"
By Scott Willis
ASCD Update
December 1994, Vol. 36, No. 10, pp. 1, 3–4.

"Choosing a Theme"
By Scott Willis
Curriculum Update
November 1992, pp. 4–5.

Designing Effective Interdisciplinary Anchors

By Sasha A. Barab and Anita Landa

When focused on a problem worth solving, interdisciplinary units provide common ground, motivate students, and offer opportunities for a multitude of learning activities and modes.

A group of high school students recently prepared environmental impact studies for their state legislature. They were so impressed with the magnitude of their responsibility to be accurate and fair in representing both environmental and economic concerns that they began to see themselves as public servants rather than students. It did not occur to them until they submitted their beautifully designed reports that they had been learning skills, facts, and principles associated with the fields of ecology, chemistry, biology, statistics, economics, government, computer applications, and graphic design.

Recent findings in cognitive neuroscience confirm what perceptive practitioners have long known: there are as many ways of learning as there are learners; and knowledge is inextricably tied to the context in which it is used. The problem is: How can one teacher, presenting one curriculum, hope to reach 20 or 30 students whose neurological makeup and life experiences vary widely?

The teacher could individualize instruction or organize students into groups with similar learning styles and life experiences. Or the teacher could answer a simple question: Outside of the classroom, how and why do these diverse learners master the vast range of information and skills needed in our astoundingly complex world?

The answer is that children learn by mobilizing their innate capacities to meet everyday challenges they perceive as meaningful. Skills and concepts are most often learned as tools to meet present demands rather than as facts to be memorized today in hopes of application tomorrow. Further, daily life is not separated into academic disciplines or divided into discrete time units; instead, the environment presents problems that one must address in an interdisciplinary, free-flowing way, usually in collaboration with peers and mentors.

These lines of reasoning point toward curriculum units that are problem-centered; interdisciplinary; presented in an interactive, cooperative format; and appeal to a multitude of students. Indeed, school districts across North America are encouraging and supporting interdisciplinary curriculums in order to respond to student diversity in all its forms—cultural, developmental, cognitive, motivational, and stylistic.

The Organizing Hub

We, our students, and our colleagues have developed interdisciplinary curriculums that not only draw upon multiple disciplines, but also transform students' appreciation of the content they are learning. We view these interdisciplinary units as Heidi Jacobs (1989) does—units in which teachers use language, principles, and methodologies associated with more than one discipline to explore a central theme, problem, issue, topic, or experience—a focus that is frequently referred to as the *hub* or organizing center.

In addition, these hubs demonstrate the relevance of mastering a set of skills and concepts. With this emphasis in mind, we have borrowed the notion of an *anchor* as a metaphor for conceiving and designing interdisciplinary units (Cognition and Technology Group at Vanderbilt [CTGV] 1993).

The most successful curricular hubs closely correspond to how the brain perceives and manipulates the environment—not to how a computer stores facts. From this perspective, the brain is continuously constructing meanings that are linked to the situations in which they are learned and used, a process that is mediated by our individual neuro-physiology and experience (Clancey, 1993; Edelman, 1992; Gazzaniga, 1995).

These findings present us with two challenges in designing interdisciplinary curricular hubs. The hub must (1) provide a meaningful *anchor*, a focused problem or question that both students and teacher can agree is worth addressing; and (2) the hub must be complex enough to accommodate a wide range of entry points and activities.

Students are the best source of topics that interest them, although they often cannot frame their ideas in ways that capture the multiple demands of successful interdisciplinary curriculums. Elementary school students along seacoasts often want to study whales; in mountainous areas, wolves are popular. Favorite middle school themes in Olympia, Washington; Hartford, Connecticut; and Independence, Missouri, include civil rights, child abuse, Native Americans, and immigration. One group of primary school students in rural Cheyenne, Wyoming, insisted on learning about spiders and butterflies, stoutly resisting efforts to expand or inte-grate their interests. By contrast, high school students' preferences tend to run toward the general and the abstract: justice, the environment, and the future.

Framing for Maximum Learning

Skillful teachers can frame these topics in ways that provide common ground, facilitate insights into why specific proficiencies and information are important, and offer ample opportunities for an abundance of learning activities and learning modes.

For example, teachers in Spokane, Wash-ington, broadened a request to study wolves to include all wild canids. They developed a series of organizing questions around other topics—pack and family structures, habitats, and relations among predators. While specific questions kept the theme

anchored to students' interests, broadening the curricular hub opened doors to disciplines and activ-ities beyond ecology and biology—to mythology, art, dance, music, anthropology, and history.

The range of activities is what serves diverse learners. For example, a suburban school included dogs in its unit on local fauna. A student with attention deficit disorder was so excited over the unit that she proceeded to track a real dog on its journeys through the neighborhood. She read Eliza-beth Marshall Thomas's *The Hidden Life of Dogs* as a guide to interpreting the dog's behavior, created a journal of the dog's life, and trained younger kids in the basics of naturalistic observation. For once, that student wandered with a purpose. For many distractable students, active experience is not just a doorway to learning; it is the only way to learn.

A Problem Worth Solving

A curricular *anchor* is a complex problem that the student acknowledges as worth solving and that validates the learning of a set of relevant skills and concepts. The notion of an anchor was developed by the Cognition and Technology Group at Vander-bilt University (CTGV, 1990, 1993). The group's extensive research suggests that carefully designed anchors help students learn techniques, facts, and ideas in long-term and transferable ways.

Anchors can be invented or natural, narrative or analytical problems, as long as they fulfill four requirements. They must:

■ capture the imagination,
■ be perceived as important by learners,
■ legitimize the disciplinary content they integrate, and
■ accommodate a variety of learning approaches.

"Rescuing Rocky," a computerized lesson developed to research the power of anchors, is an example of an invented anchor (Barab et al. 1996). The lesson is presented through text, pictures, videos, and animated stories. It begins with a one-minute QuickTime video explaining that a monkey, Rocky, is dying of simian AIDS contracted in a government lab experiment. The video informs viewers that a scientist in the Brazilian rain forests has discovered a cure for AIDS, but her research data and the area of rain forest where she had been working was destroyed by fire. Just before the disaster, she had written to a colleague, giving clues to the AIDS cure.

Students read the scientist's letter and decide which information they would like to explore to regenerate the cure themselves. To solve the anchor problem, they must travel to the rain forest, and to do that they must learn about customs, international laws, and exchange rates. To experiment with various plants and insects, they must learn about viruses, immunizations, AIDS, simian immunodeficiency virus, deforestation, plants and animals of the rain forest, ethics, and chemical interactions. They do not learn these concepts as objective facts to be memorized; they learn them as important tools that they must understand and properly apply to save Rocky.

Significantly, students learning the content to address the anchor problem scored higher on achievement questions and evidenced more transfer of knowledge than did students who studied the information without the anchor. More important, students learning in the context of an engaging anchor made connections among various disciplinary concepts, even seeing relations between the computerized lesson and other lessons, and between the lesson and personal experiences. For example, one student told us that his mother worked in the "underground," helping to make available various medicines for AIDS patients who could not afford the expensive new combinations of drugs.

An example of a more natural anchor is a Bill of Rights that a group of middle school students recently created. The students enthusiastically

researched the struggles of Martin Luther King Jr. and studied the U.S. Constitution and the *Sheff v. O'Neill* case, in which the U.S. Supreme Court ruled on equal educational opportunity in the students' local community and more globally. They learned information and skills from an array of disciplines—history, government, law, economics, philosophy, communications, computers, desktop publishing, and mathematics.

These imaginative projects suggest several questions to ask when designing interdisciplinary anchors/hubs:

1. Will the anchor require students to draw on principles and skills associated with more than one discipline?

2. Will both students and teachers view the content as a legitimate area to study?

3. Will the anchor generate developmentally appropriate activities?

4. Will the activities provide entry points and opportunities for success for learners with diverse learning styles and cultural experiences?

Orchestrating the Disciplines

No matter how well integrated interdisciplinary curriculums are, in most, a single broad domain serves as the mortar that holds the project together. Can you teach physics while studying wild canids? Sure, anything that moves follows the laws of motion. But when animals are at the core of the curriculum, the life sciences demand and deserve centrality.

In a middle school unit on electricity and electric invention, physics and mechanics were central, although teachers were able to include math (measurement), blueprint design, history, and writing. Similarly, an ongoing land management project in a rural school is basically a schoolwide ecology or environmental studies program. But the project, in which students are implementing the state conservation plan in several acres of meadow and woodland, also legitimately includes plant and animal science, forestry and horticulture, and photography and surveying.

In a multi-age project, students have turned the walls of their school into a museum, reproducing works from cave paintings to Picasso and accompanying them with historical and biographical information. This curriculum was built on art and art history, but it easily accommodated many other subjects—cultural and political history, biographical research, writing and editing, video production, business skills, and all the construction skills. Visitors may view and purchase a video about the museum and buy postcards and reproductions of the art works. Each year, students add a new era or culture and teachers are expanding the disciplinary reach by including crafts and industrial design.

In striving for an interdisciplinary approach, the question is not how many disciplines one can integrate, but rather, "Will the unit provide a diversity of learners opportunities to try difficult tasks and learn new skills in a motivating and rewarding context?" The unit on electricity, for example, provided a discouraged 13-year-old with a chance to develop and display his strong visual and spatial abilities. It also required him to use language, one of his weaker areas, to write up experiments and display projects. His homeroom teacher reported that he "went from doing no work to completing all his work." Classmates whose primary intelligence was musical or verbal (as described by Howard Gardner, 1983), didn't make great leaps in the electricity unit. But they did experience a more narrative, less narrowly logical and mathematical way of learning subject matter that they ordinarily did not find congenial.

Structuring and Scheduling

Although interdisciplinary units are a creative and effective way of motivating students and engaging more learners, they present obstacles—both practical and philosophical—to designing and implementing them. Legitimate questions include:
■ *What happens to "the structure of the disciplines" that Jerome Bruner (1968) has described so eloquently?* If canids or electricity are the real topic, how can math or music be taught in a properly structured sequence? Here are two suggestions.

First, teachers should design interdisciplinary units to follow the sequence of the disciplines they integrate. In other words, 5th graders publishing a newspaper would circulate and analyze a survey to determine how many copies to print; would decide how many 500-page reams of paper to order given the size of the page and number of issues; and would create a budget, estimating their expenses and generating a per-paper cost. Seventh graders would need a project that calls for a more complex sequence of math concepts and skills, perhaps a design-and-build project that combines geometry with formulas for determining the properties and capabilities of various building materials.

To preserve the structure of the appropriate disciplines for middle school and high school, the teacher could follow the Federated Learning Communities model that Gabelnick and colleagues (1990) described. The model weaves the integrating theme or anchor into several existing courses. The model also calls for a seminar or forum that helps students integrate information and ideas from the various disciplines into the curricular hub and provides a setting for special projects and presentations.

Racial prejudice and world hunger are two popular anchors in this model because their urgency

travels easily across disciplines. The unit on environmental impact studies was also taught in a Learning Communities format. Learning communities often result in student-generated projects that are time-consuming and hard to administer, but worth their weight in learning opportunities and public relations.

■ *What happens to the school schedule?* A self-contained classroom easily accommodates interdisciplinary units. In the upper grades, however, where a whole school is scheduled in 40- or 50-minute blocks, scheduling can be more difficult. The Learning Communities model eliminates scheduling problems, but does require the school to set aside one or two periods each week for the seminars.

Another scheduling strategy for middle and high schools is to combine class periods, creating a double-time block during which students can consider the theme or anchor from two disciplinary perspectives. One example is an AIDS unit that a joint history and English class designed. The students imported the information they needed through guest lectures, videos, and field trips, while concentrating on the historical and communications aspects of understanding and preventing the disease. They prepared two AIDS curriculums, one for younger students and the other for their parents.

■ *How can teachers find time for interdisciplinary curriculums?* We concede that these curriculums are time-consuming, and we have no easy answers. We do know that many teachers use this approach despite the time it takes. They do so for several reasons: It is exhilarating; it brings their creativity into play; it enables them to collaborate imaginatively with colleagues; and it is a reliable way to bring all students into the circle of successful learners. ■

References

Barab, S.A., B.R. Fajen, J.M. Kulikowich, and M.F. Young. (1996). "Assessing Navigation through Pathfinder: Learning from Dribble Files." *Journal of Educational Computing Research* 15, 3: 175–195.

Bruner, J.S. (1968). *Toward a Theory of Instruction.* New York: W.W. Norton & Company, Inc.

Clancey, W.J. (1993). "Situated Action: A Neuro-psychological Interpretation Response to Vera and Simon." *Cognitive Science* 17, 1: 87–117.

Cognition and Technology Group at Vanderbilt. (June 1990). "Anchored Instruction and Its Relationship to Situated Cognition." *Educational Researcher* 19, 6: 2–10.

Cognition and Technology Group at Vanderbilt. (March 1993). "Anchored Instruction and Situated Cognition Revisited." *Educational Technology* 33, 3: 52–70.

Edelman, G.M. (1992). *Bright Air, Brilliant Fire: On the Matter of the Mind.* New York: Basic Books.

Gabelnick, F., J. MacGregor, R. Mathews, and B. Smith. (1990). *Learning Communities: Connections Among Students, Faculty, and Disciplines.* San Francisco: Jossey Bass.

Gardner, H. (1983). *Frames of Mind.* New York: Basic Books.

Gazzaniga, M.S. (1995). *The Cognitive Neurosciences.* Cambridge, Mass.: MIT Press.

Jacobs, H. (1989). *Interdisciplinary Curriculum: Design and Implementation.* Alexandria, Va.: ASCD.

Sasha A. Barab is an interdisciplinary consultant to a Hartford middle school and an instructor in the Department of Educational Psychology, Box U-4, University of Connecticut, Storrs, CT 06269-2004. E-mail: barab@Uconnvm.UConn.Edu

Anita Landa is an Assistant Professor, Peaceable Schools Masters Program, Cambridge, MA 02318-2790.

Teaching for Understanding—Within and Across the Disciplines

By Howard Gardner and Veronica Boix-Mansilla

The disciplines are the most useful means for illuminating those issues that have perennially engaged the curiosity of thoughtful human beings.

As they enter middle and high school, students are expected to understand central concepts in several disciplines. While students may succeed in "parroting back" phrases from lectures and texts, they often falter when asked to apply their understanding to new situations. What does it take to demonstrate understanding within and across disciplines? Consider the many different ways to approach the following hypothetical but plausible situations:

■ *The New York Times* announced that the Queen of England has stepped down from her throne and at the same time has disestablished the House of Windsor. The English monarchy is at an end.

■ *The New England Journal of Medicine* has published a study in which two groups of elementary school students were randomly assigned to two after-school programs: indoor gymnasium sports and personal computer work. Twice as many students in the first group contracted colds. The speculation is that after-school athletics may be injurious to one's health.

Wearing the hat of the disciplinarian, we can consider our first example as drawn from history or social studies and the second from biology or general science. Either account could serve as the point of departure of a set of lessons in appropriate high school classes. If reworded, they could be used with students at virtually any grade level. The first account—which could also refer to the death of a president or the deposing of any kind of leader—

raises questions such as "What makes a boss a boss?" or "Why do all civilizations have hierarchies of authority?" The second account could be reformulated to describe any source of disease and to encourage reflections about what keeps us healthy, what is illness, and how to prevent it.

Here we attempt to place current efforts at teaching for understanding into a sharper perspective by considering the way in which this performance view plays out in different disciplines.

Understanding Within the Disciplines

The four-part framework developed by our Teaching for Understanding group is deliberately broad enough to cover the range of disciplines. At the same time, however, all disciplines are not equal. In fact, distinct disciplines have developed over the ages precisely because they allow scholars and students to take different kinds of perspectives and actions in order to elucidate specific kinds of phenomena.

Consider our opening examples. In each case, we are dealing with a central concept: (1) injury to the body politic, and (2) injury to the physical body. Analysis and evaluation of concepts are legitimate tacks in both examples.

In other respects, however, the disciplinary terrains prove quite different. For instance, to gain relevant expertise in our abdication situation, students might draw on knowledge about British history and its current form of government, as well as the legal and symbolic implications of the abolition of monarchy. Students can "perform" their understandings in any number of ways—ranging from a comparison of the situation at the time of the beheading of King Charles I or the abdication of Edward VIII, to a hypothetical argument in a local pub about the abolition, to the creation of a diagram of the new governmental organization.

By their very nature, historical phenomena are unique. One can compare abdications and beheadings, but they are never the same. When dealing with individual personalities, varying contexts, and dynamic events, the complexity of the events can never be mastered nor the consequences predicted. Finally, events in this sphere take on symbolic as well as literal/legal importance. While in practice the British monarchy has little authority, in actuality it assumes significant symbolic power. A disciplinary understanding of the possible impacts of disestablishment on British public life is grounded in these specific features of historical events.

In contrast to the historical example, the realm of health and illness, at least in principle, should be open to explanation and prediction. This realm lends itself to the development of models of what causes illness and the testing of the models through experimentation. A well-founded model is able to predict results across diverse populations. Moreover, explicit methodologies exist for mounting experiments and for analyzing data, ones that can be used by anyone schooled in science. Consequently, in the case of colds among athletes, students might gain relevant expertise by drawing on knowledge about health and illness, including bacterial and viral theories of infection, as well as understandings of the nature of scientific hypotheses, experimental designs, and inferences from data. To demonstrate their understanding, students might conduct similar experiments, perform retrospective examinations of the incidence and plausible causes of their own recent colds, or construct rival models of disease.

From Common Sense to Interdisciplinary Study

So far, we have dealt with what might be called "normal" disciplinary work at the secondary level. We have assumed that there are classes that deal with historical-political studies, those that deal with scientific inquiry, and a set of roles and performances appropriate to students in those respective classes.

But we have also argued that younger students

could approach the questions raised in appropriate ways. To illustrate, we single out four stages, corresponding roughly to different points in the growth patterns of students (Gardner and Boix-Mansilla 1993).

1. Common sense. Novices fruitfully consider generative questions by relying on their intuitive theories of the world—their natural theories of mind, matter, and life (Gardner 1991). Students as young as 5 or 6 can consider what it means to be a leader and then voluntarily or involuntarily to renounce one's position as boss. They can consider what would happen if the teacher or the boss stepped down and no one took his or her place. Adults can ask young students to draw on their own theories of power—the person who is strongest, loudest, bossiest, or the person chosen by someone even more powerful—to debate these issues.

These same students can also be guided into discussions of health. All youngsters are interested in their bodies—what makes them strong, weak, sick, or healthy. They can apply their own naive theories—you are sick because you were bad, because you sat near someone who was sick, because you did not wash your hands—to new events, including the appearance of a new sickness or a new cure. Note that in these cases, it is not important that students espouse the "right theories," but that they draw fully on their own ideas in an effort to make sense—to perform their understandings—of intriguing phenomena.

2. Protodisciplinary knowledge. Even in the absence of formal disciplinary study, students in our culture pick up certain moves that are made by systematic thinkers—through, for example, the media, debates among peers, and partial understanding of texts. Long before they have heard of college catalogues, and despite the movie *JFK*, students in the late primary or early middle grades begin to appreciate the difference between a historical account (what actually happened) and a literary account (a description invented for aesthetic purposes). By the same token, they begin to distinguish claims that are based on conviction or prejudice from claims based on empirical evidence, which itself can be confirmed or questioned.

At this stage, youngsters can proceed in a more sophisticated way. They can read historical or scientific accounts, summarize them, conduct further research, and debate the validity of various claims. And they can engage in projects—such as holding a mock trial or conducting a survey—that introduce them naturally to the tools of the disciplines.

3. Disciplinary knowledge. By late middle school and thereafter, students do most work under the rubric of classical disciplines, such as history, literature, and the sciences. Because it is fashionable to look askance at the disciplines, we feel it is important to make two points. First, disciplines are not the same as subjects. Disciplines constitute the most sophisticated ways yet developed for thinking about and investigating issues that have long fascinated and perplexed thoughtful individuals; subject matters are devices for organizing schedules and catalogues. Second, disciplines represent the principal ways in which individuals transcend ignorance. While disciplines can blind or sway, they become, when used relevantly, our keenest lenses on the world.

When well taught, students are introduced to the disciplines in several ways. First, they observe teachers or experts who embody the practices of the disciplines. Second, students behold and create exhibitions that capture the accumulated wisdom of the discipline. Third, students encounter the concepts, theories, and methods that disciplinarians have evolved over the years, and receive ample opportunities to put them into practice. Only through such sustained work—work that is "disciplined" in both senses of the term—may students acquire the expertise that we have described.

4. Beyond disciplinary knowledge. Even as it is now fashionable to critique the disciplines, it is trendy to advocate "interdisciplinary" work. At its best, interdisciplinary work is indeed vital and impressive. However, such work can only be legitimately attempted if one has already mastered at least portions of the specific disciplines. Unfortunately, much of what is termed "interdisciplinary" work is actually predisciplinary work—that is, work based on common sense, not on the mastery and integration of a number of component disciplines.

Those who have slogged through a number of specific disciplines are in a privileged position. They can conduct *multidisciplinary* work in which, for example, they look at the abdication of King Edward VIII as portrayed in art, literature, history, and philosophy. They can undertake *interdisciplinary* work, in which they consider the concept of health in terms of both medicine and individual psychology, and then synthesize these perspectives in coming up with a more general account. They can carry on *metadisciplinary* work, in which they compare the practices of particular disciplines, as we have done earlier in this article. And they can engage in *transdisciplinary* work, where they examine a concept, like "body," as it appears in political and in physical discourse.

Disciplinary Powers and Limitations

In our view, the disciplines are the most useful means for illuminating those generative issues that have perennially engaged the curiosity of thoughtful human beings. What in the past was approached first through common sense, and later through art, mythology, and religion, can now be approached as well through systematic studies, such as political science or medical experimentation.

While we should be respectful of disciplines, we should remain aware of at least three limitations:

1. Far from being ends in themselves, the disciplines are means for answering generative "essential" questions. Indeed, armed with the disciplines and with the possibility of interdisciplinary work, individuals are in the best position to revisit these essential questions and to arrive at their own, often deeply personal answers.

2. Disciplines are differently transfigured, depending on purpose and developmental levels. For elementary education, it may be enough to separate out the arts and humanities, on the one hand, and the experimental sciences on the other. At the high school level, a distinction into three or four disciplinary terrains probably suffices (Sizer 1992). And at the university level, a quite fine differentiation and articulation among disciplines is appropriate.

3. All disciplinary boundaries are tentative. Disciplines have not been, and probably never will be, marked in stone. Rather, they develop out of specific conditions, and as these conditions change, boundaries are redrawn. Moreover, even within the most established disciplines, serious disagreements exist with respect to content, methods, and scope. The dynamism of disciplines reflects the always growing, ever-changing nature of knowledge.

Assessment Within and Across the Disciplines

Some aspects of assessment are appropriate for all disciplines, while others turn out to be far more specific to particular disciplinary practices. At the generic level, each discipline features certain characteristic roles—the historical analyst, the designer of experiments—and certain characteristic performances or exhibitions—a historical account, an experimental write-up. Students need to be immersed in instances of these roles and performances of understanding, particularly as they are practiced by proficient individuals.

But even the best instances do not suffice. It does not benefit the rookie pianist to hear Arthur Rubinstein or the novice tennis player only to witness Martina Navratilova. Rather, students must

encounter individual benchmarks on the trail from novice to expert, as well as road maps of how to get from one milestone to the next. Given these landmarks, along with ample opportunity to perform their understanding with appropriate feedback, most individuals should be able to steadily enhance their competence in any discipline.

Of course, disciplines lend themselves to different kinds of roles and performances. To read texts critically, in the manner of a historian, is a quite different matter than to design a crucial experiment and analyze data relevant to competing models of an infectious process. Different disciplines call on different analytic styles, approaches to problem solving and findings, temperaments, and intelligences. Therefore, a keen assessment must be alert to these disciplinary differences. By the same token, an effective teacher should help youngsters to appreciate that what counts as cause and effect, data and explanation, use of language and argument, varies across the disciplines.

From Disciplinary to Personal Knowledge

All individuals the world over, not just knowledgeable people, ask generative questions. Children do not ask about the meaning of life and death or good and bad merely because others talk about these issues. Rather, these questions arise spontaneously, prompting children to pose them in their own way and to come up with imaginative answers. The disciplines, individually and jointly, offer the best current efforts to approach, and to supply, provisional answers for these enduring questions. As we saw in our two simple examples (about abdication and illness), just as questions come from different points and lead to different kinds of answers, the disciplines themselves have disparate roots and lead, by varying routes, to different kinds of accounts.

Drawing on the disciplines, we should find it possible to mount increasingly comprehensive approaches to generative questions—approaches that are appropriate to particular contexts and populations. In the end, however, we need to keep in mind that the disciplines remain but the means for tackling these questions. The most important answers are those that individuals ultimately craft for themselves, based on their disciplinary understandings, their personal experiences, and their own feelings and values. ■

References

Gardner, H. (1991). *The Unschooled Mind.* Basic Books: New York.

Gardner, H., and V. Boix-Mansilla. (1993). "Teaching for Understanding in the Disciplines ... and Beyond." Paper prepared for the conference Teachers' Conceptions of Knowledge, Tel Aviv, Israel, June 1993. To be published in the Proceedings.

Sizer, T. (1992). *Horace's School.* Boston: Houghton Mifflin.

Howard Gardner is Professor of Education and Co-Director of Project Zero at the Harvard Graduate School of Education; **Veronica Boix-Mansilla** is a doctoral student and Researcher at Project Zero and the Harvard Graduate School of Education. Both may be reached at 323 Longfellow Hall, Appian Way, Cambridge, MA 02138.

Courting Controversy
How to Build Interdisciplinary Units

By Jackie Williams and Terry Deal Reynolds

When teachers build interdisciplinary thematic units around hot local issues, the result, said one student, is "learn, learn, learn."

As 25 6th graders from a small school in an affluent area of Asheville, North Carolina, stepped off the two new school vans, the rural surroundings looked somewhat foreboding. It was an overcast day, and in the dim light, the plain school building before them appeared shabby and in need of repair. The smell reeking from the Pigeon River across the street augmented the dismal atmosphere. And then there was a daunting sign, "Warning: Dioxin."

The Asheville students entered the small country school, which serves 70 children in grades K–8. The visiting students were amazed to see birds flying freely to their nests in the open hallways.

In the classrooms, the visitors met their hosts. At first, both groups of students were reluctant to mix. They sat awkwardly in pairs and small groups. At the teachers' encouragement, the students began to converse shyly, the guests dutifully asking questions and taking notes on their partners' replies.

To break the ice still further, the principal of the school (who also taught 7th and 8th grades) persuaded a few of his students to perform a rap that they had written about their community's problems. The lively beat and stirring message soon led to animated conversation between the two groups of students.

As the 90-minute visit progressed, the children gradually became engrossed in a variety of activities. Some walked along the river with host students. Others chatted in groups on the floor of the classrooms. Three students were fascinated by scrapbooks in the school library. The task-oriented few taped interviews with teachers.

On the surface, the visit appeared to be a casual exchange between students from different locales. The young people from Asheville, however, actually learned a great deal about life in a rural Tennessee town. They heard how the lifeblood of the community, the Pigeon River, is contaminated by toxic chemicals, often has an unnatural coffee-like color, and always smells like rotten eggs due to the wastewater discharge from a paper mill 50 miles upstream. On discovering that many of the 600 residents suspect that the flood of pollution is implicated in the cancer-related deaths of loved ones, the students sensed the frustration that stems from years of unsuccessful attempts to get people to listen and care and act. Students also began to grasp the difficulty of influencing the large, powerful paper industry.

Back at their home school the next day, the students eagerly began to write about their experiences. They portrayed the individuals they interviewed, describing not only physical attributes, but personalities and attitudes. They accurately depicted the school, community, and lifestyles encountered. They ventured beyond interview transcripts and observations to interject their own thoughts. Their powerful, moving documentaries revealed a genuine understanding of one side of a complex environmental issue involving many different points of view.

But this assignment required more than clear images and candor. Before the trip, the interviewers had been (1) primed to take complete notes, which would later be organized and summarized; (2) instructed to write with great detail and precision, making sure of all the facts used; and (3) urged to use quotations to emphasize certain points or add interest to their stories.

Integrating Several Subjects

This 6th grade trip to rural Tennessee was not an isolated event, but one of the many hands-on experiences in a 12-week interdisciplinary unit. Designed to make each student an expert on paper making, stream pollution, and the controversy whirling around dumping toxic wastes into a previously scenic river, the unit also prompts students to learn and use important concepts in science, social studies, language arts, and mathematics.

Teachers from each of the four subject areas devoted a great deal of time and effort to planning the unit. When implemented, however, it unfolded so beautifully that it surprised even the most optimistic members of the team, prompted further curriculum development, and led a movement to change the entire middle school program to one organized around interdisciplinary thematic units and team teaching.

Throughout the implementation of the unit, the teachers made a point of not differentiating among the subject areas. During the planning phase, though, each of the teachers represented his or her discipline, and each had two clear-cut responsibilities: to make sure that content and skills from each subject were developed during the unit and to provide suggestions as to how this might be done.

In *science*, the unit activities came to center on river pollution, with a special emphasis on wastewater discharge from pulp and paper mills. A state environmental management official spoke to the students about the facts in the Pigeon River pollution and explained the system used to monitor stream pollution. Prior to their trip, the students practiced stream sampling. During the trip, they compared their own data to results from the state regulatory agencies.

Students heard a former paper industry executive talk about paper making, and then they toured a mill. On their return to school, the students tried making paper. After experimenting for nearly a week, exuberant voices rang through the school: "It worked! We *made* paper!"

At the end of the unit, students completed an extensive written exam. The science teacher said that he had never seen such a thorough grasp of complex scientific concepts in a group of 6th graders.

In *social studies*, the students studied the issue of toxic waste dumping. First, they examined files on the subject in the local library. Thereafter, they followed the news for updates. In the process, they began to understand the political, economic, and social implications of a large industry where jobs, livelihoods, and consumer convenience have to be weighed against the environment, health, and the preservation of natural resources.

In perceiving these trade-offs, students learned that there are many sides to an issue. It also became clear that in order to look at a problem objectively, facts must be disentangled from opinions. Another key revelation was that responsible action can only be taken if citizens are informed. For their part, the students became keenly aware and involved. In fact, by the end of the unit, the students knew more about this local controversy than many of their well-informed parents and teachers.

Meanwhile, the *language arts* teachers jumped at every chance to involve the students in authentic communication. Guest speakers, tours, interviews, and presentations provided wonderful occasions to practice the listening and note-taking necessary to prepare oral and written presentations.

Writing assignments included an exposition called "How to Make Paper," interview write-ups, and position papers.

Reading played a key part in the entire process, too. From newspaper articles, notes, and handouts, learners developed their own chronology of important events. Weekly vocabulary lists included paper-making terms, such as *lignin, tannin,* and *dioxin.*

Speaking opportunities abounded as well. The 6th graders became quite adept at interviewing techniques, and through dramatic portrayals of fictional characters who might have been involved in the controversy, the students stated their own views and responded to others' opinions. Each student also participated in a dialogue as part of the final examination.

Mathematics skills were acquired and applied during the stream-sampling efforts, since collecting and manipulating the data (on, for instance, stream depth, velocity, and temperature) required computation and the application of mathematical formulas. To help plan the overnight field trip to the paper mill and the rural Tennessee school, students were called upon to develop personal budgets. They also had to manage their money and record their expenses during the trip.

Forming Interdisciplinary Teams

One of the best ways to integrate the curriculum is to pull all of the subject-area teachers together to develop thematic units. The team can look first at the characteristics and needs of their learners—academic, social/emotional, and physical—and then design specific units with clear objectives and appropriate activities tailored to meet the identified needs.

Each teacher on the team contributes to the planning and thus develops a sense of ownership for the unit. The team members share the responsibility for setting up special activities, collecting materials, and contacting community resource people.

One giant hurdle that the interdisciplinary team must clear is the temptation to force integration of the curriculum by stringing existing activities together. The inclination is understandable— any veteran educator has accumulated mounds of teaching materials that save time and effort.

All the same, if team members are to focus on a fresh new theme, they must let go of old, comfortable props. Planning all-new activities may prove tedious and time-consuming, but the ultimate rewards make the effort worthwhile.

Choosing a Theme

The success of an interdisciplinary unit depends on a good choice of themes. For several reasons, we have found a controversial local issue makes a good topic. First, it ignites student interest in ways that other studies can't. Students begin to examine the needs of their own community through previously unexplored sources of information and find many ways to become involved and make contributions. Through interviews of local citizens and leaders, students come to see that no problem is as simple or one-sided as it appears and that few problems have perfect or easy solutions.

In addition, local issues present many ways to bring the community into the classroom; such opportunities include guest speakers, demonstrations, and displays of student research results. Finally, community resources are close—often just a phone call away. Parents, especially, often become so enthused that they offer assistance or just find common ground for talking with their child.

The themes for an effective unit must be relevant and thought-provoking, for if the topic is meaningful for others in the school and community, people will want to hear what the students have to say about it—and nothing motivates like a captivated audience.

And, while it is important for each of the subject-area experts to make sure that activities are included from each discipline, learners, too, can influence decisions about themes or activities. The students might brainstorm ideas and discuss them prior to the teaching team's decision, or the process could work in reverse, with the team generating ideas for the students to discuss and choose.

No Problem-Free Units

The development of an interdisciplinary unit is unlikely to be problem-free. The example that we have described was no exception!

Initially, there were some doubts about the value of such a project. Our team also experienced some typical problems: philosophical differences; scheduling conflicts; perceptions that some members were not doing their fair share of the work; and a harried sense of *too-much-to-do-and-nowhere-near-enough-time-to-do-it*.

Nonetheless, all the members of the team are now convinced that the benefits of this powerful learning experience cannot be matched by any departmentalized teaching approach.

Maybe one of the reasons for the teachers' ultimate commitment to the concept is the way students responded. After the two-day field trip, one student reported back to an administrator. "It was great!" she declared. She had only one complaint: "All we did was learn, learn, learn!" ■

Jackie Williams and **Terry Deal Reynolds** recently taught grades 6 and 7 at the Carolina Day School in Asheville, North Carolina. They are now curriculum consultants who promote teaching language arts through hands-on experiences.

© Association for Supervision and Curriculum Development

Planning for Curriculum Integration

By Heidi Hayes Jacobs

Using the four-phase action plan described here, districts can effectively create multidisciplinary units and see them through to successful adoption.

To develop an interdisciplinary curriculum, a district needs an action plan. Here is such a plan, based on extensive field work. The plan's four phases—conducting internal and external action research, developing a proposal, implementing and monitoring a pilot unit, and adopting the program—can be accomplished over a three-year period.

Phase I: Conducting Action Research

The time frame for carrying out research is six months to a year. During this phase, staff members concentrate on learning more about their current curriculum as well as about best practices from the field.

Internal research. Research is conducted internally by small groups of teachers assembled by grade levels, departments, or interdisciplinary teams. Using the school calendar, they plot month-by-month the units of study they teach. If each teacher comes prepared with his or her individual monthly outline, compiling the information takes only a few hours.

With information for an entire year at their fingertips, teachers can:

(1) discover when students are studying various units in their subjects;

(2) align subjects that would mutually benefit from concurrent teaching (Jacobs, 1989);

(3) eliminate repetition from year to year;

(4) identify possibilities for multidisciplinary or interdisciplinary units of study (Jacobs, 1989); and

(5) target units that lend themselves to performance-based assessment of specific skills and concepts.

External research. External research extends staff members' awareness of relevant work in the larger education community. Through conferences, readings, site visits, inservice courses, and voluntary study groups, they study best practices and options for curriculum reform. Regional service centers, state educational departments, national education organizations, and universities are excellent sources for learning about desirable practices.

Topics that teachers often choose for further research include team building, curriculum design, scheduling alternatives, evaluation approaches, and writing across the content areas. Investigation of these areas can be helpful to teachers as they develop interdisciplinary programs.

Phase II: Developing a Proposal

Phase two, proposal development, usually takes from two to four months during the first year of planning. One of the first tasks is to assess potential areas for multidisciplinary or interdisciplinary units.

For their first effort, most schools decide to upgrade an existing unit of study through collaboration between disciplines. The length of the pilot is usually from two to six weeks. If the proposal is to be effective, the most motivated and capable staff members should be involved in its design. Further, the proposal should specify evaluation procedures, budget, timelines, and teachers' responsibilities.

Two dangers inherent in a pilot are its experimental cast and its peripheral nature (Jacobs, 1989). A strong long-term agenda can allay these problems. Creating an interdisciplinary proposal should not be seen as an enrichment event; ultimately, the goal is for the pilot to become part of the program, not a passing experience. As a middle school teacher put it, "We're going to try this science and English unit on the ethics of experimentation because we believe it's better than what we're doing now separately."

After the proposal has been written and

reviewed at the building and district levels, it's time to try the unit in the classroom.

Phase III:
Implementing and Monitoring the Pilot

The third phase, implementing and monitoring the pilot unit, takes place during the second year of the plan. Most units run from two to six weeks.

During the pilot, teachers evaluate decision-making procedures, relationships between team members, time allotted for implementation, adequacy of resource materials, and political considerations. A frequent outcome of their efforts, according to teachers, is the satisfaction of collegial collaboration. As Leiberman and Miller suggest, "it is the personal interaction rather than instructional interaction that is most valued" (1990, p. 159).

The group members also meet regularly to assess the impact of the pilot unit on students. If they have devised outcome-based assessments for the pilot, they now have critical feedback about student growth.

The key to the pilot's success is the data collected through the monitoring procedures. From this wealth of information, the staff then plans revisions to the unit's design or to conditions that influence its effectiveness.

Phase IV: Adopting the Program

During the third year of the plan, staff members are prepared to make revisions to the program, based on the data collected in the pilot phase, and then adopt it as a permanent part of the curriculum. There is no time in a school year to add more curriculum. So, in order to adopt the pilot, they must replace whatever was offered previously. For example, the high school course guide will now state that there is a 9th grade Humanities course rather than separate English, social studies, and arts courses. A pilot can easily dissipate unless it is elevated to program status.

Looking Ahead

Eventually, staff members will want to examine the new unit for ways to expand it throughout the system. Over two to three years, schools can make steady and meaningful curriculum reform. A successful interdisciplinary pilot can spearhead systematic examination of scheduling, teaming, and evaluation procedures.

By following an action plan based on solid research, a powerful pilot, and thoughtful monitoring, district planners can guide a unit through to successful program adoption. ■

References

Jacobs, H.H. (1989). "Design Options for an Integrated Curriculum." In *Interdisciplinary Curriculum: Design and Implementation*, edited by H. H. Jacobs, pp. 13-24. Alexandria, Va.: Association for Supervision and Curriculum Development.

Leiberman, A., and L. Miller. (1990). "The Social Realities of Teaching." In *Schools as Collaborative Cultures: Creating the Future Now*, edited by A. Leiberman. Bristol, Pa.: Falmer Press.

Heidi Hayes Jacobs is Professor, Teachers College, Columbia University, Box 31, New York, NY 10027.

Example of Calendar Curriculum Mapping

Grade 6	February	March	April	May	June
English/ Language Arts	*Sarah Plain and Tall*	Wilson's Letter and Diaries of Immigrants		*Diary of Anne Franke*	
Social Studies	The Westward Movement	The Industrial Revolution; World War I		World War II	
Mathematics	Fractions Roman Numerals	Metrics Compare Bases		Percents Geometric Shapes	Scale Area
Science	Matter and Enery	Electricity ⟵	Weather	Magnetism ⟶	
Art	Color Western Landscapes	Shape; Cubists Picasso, Gris		Photography: Documentary Purposes	

A 6th grade team begins interdisciplinary planning by plotting the topics teachers teach month-by-month.

A Caveat: Curriculum Integration Isn't Always a Good Idea

By Jere Brophy and Janet Alleman

Just because an activity crosses subject-matter lines does not make it worthwhile; it must also help accomplish important educational goals.

Curriculum integration is sometimes necessary to teach about topics that cut across or transcend school subjects. Even when integration is not necessary, it is often desirable, as when content drawn from one subject is used to enrich the teaching of another (period artwork used in history) or when skills learned in one subject are used to process or apply information learned in another (debates or report writing in social studies). However, curriculum integration is not an end in itself but a means for accomplishing basic educational goals. Furthermore, recommended activities may not help achieve those goals, nor are they always implemented effectively.

We offer this caveat because, in the course of examining recent elementary social studies series, we saw many suggestions made in the name of integration that we consider counterproductive. Too often, activities described as ways to integrate social studies with other subjects either lack educational value in any subject or promote progress toward significant goals in another subject but not in social studies.

Many of these activities are pointless busywork (alphabetizing the state capitals). Others may have value as language arts activities but don't belong in social studies curriculum (exercises that use social studies content but focus on pluralizing nouns).

Moreover, many suggested activities require time-consuming artistic or construction work. Some of these develop—or at least allow for—opportunities to use social studies knowledge (constructing maps of the school), but others simply lack educa-

tional value (carving pumpkins to look like U.S. presidents). The same is true of various role-play, simulation, collage, and scrapbook activities.

So-called integration activities sometimes even distort social studies content. For example, a unit on pioneer life includes a sequencing-skills exercise built around five steps in building log cabins. Three of these five steps are arbitrarily imposed rather than logically necessary. The authors apparently included this exercise not because it developed key knowledge about pioneer life, but because they wanted to put an exercise in sequential ordering somewhere in the curriculum.

Ill-conceived integration ideas also sometimes require students to do things that are strange, difficult, or even impossible. One activity calls for students to use pantomime to communicate one of the six reasons for the Constitution as stated in its preamble. We do not think that social studies time should be spent practicing pantomime skills, but even if we did, we would select a more appropriate subject for pantomime than reasons for the Constitution.

Finally, suggested activities sometimes call for students to do things they are not prepared to do, either because the task is ambiguous (drawing a hungry face) or because it requires them to use knowledge that has not been taught in the curriculum and is not likely to have been acquired elsewhere (having 1st graders role-play scenes from Mexico when all they have learned about Mexico is its location on a map).

In view of these problems, educators should consider integration a potential tool that is feasible and desirable in some situations but not in all. An activity is appropriate because it promotes progress toward significant educational goals, not merely because it cuts across subject-matter lines. Furthermore, in assessing the time spent in integrated activities versus subject-area ones, educators should weigh the cost-effectiveness of the activities in accomplishing each subject's major goals.

Before we have students engage in activities designed to promote curriculum integration, let's apply criteria:

1. Activities should be educationally significant, ones desirable even if they did not include the integration feature.

2. Activities should foster, rather than disrupt or nullify, accomplishment of major goals in each subject area. ■

Author's note: This work is sponsored in part by the Institute for Research on Teaching, College of Education, Michigan State University. The institute is funded from a variety of federal, state, and private sources, including the U.S. Department of Education and Michigan State University. The opinions expressed here do not necessarily reflect the position, policy, or endorsement of the funding agencies.

Jere Brophy is Co-Director of the Institute for Research on Teaching and Distinguished Professor, Department of Teacher Education, Michigan State University, College of Education, Erickson Hall, East Lansing, MI 48824-1034. **Janet Alleman** is Professor, Department of Teacher Education, Michigan State University, same address.

Refocusing the Curriculum
Making Interdisciplinary Efforts Work

By Scott Willis

Unlike some other trends in teaching, interdisciplinary education has captured and held the interest of teachers. What accounts for the lasting appeal of interdisciplinary teaching?

One reason is that it allows teachers to organize the curriculum around themes, problems, or essential questions that students find more engaging than discipline-bound instruction.

"It's the natural way that human beings learn," says Suzanne Krogh of Western Washington University, author of *The Integrated Early Childhood Curriculum*. Daily life constantly calls on us to cross disciplines, she notes. When buying a car, for example, a consumer must read about different cars (English), analyze numerical data (math), negotiate with sellers (social skills), and so on. Schools shouldn't always break life experiences into fragmented subject areas, Krogh believes—and many educators today agree with her.

But interdisciplinary teaching represents a major departure from past practice. How can educators ensure that efforts to blend the subject areas are successful?

When planning interdisciplinary curriculum, teachers should be sure to "make it meaningful to the kids," advises Joan Grady, a senior program associate with the Mid-continent Regional Educational Laboratory (McREL) in Aurora, Colo. Teachers should tap into local issues, Grady suggests. If students can see the relevance to their own lives, they will put more effort into their schoolwork.

Grady offers examples of schools where teachers have successfully engaged students in real issues:

■ At a high school in North Dakota, teachers of physics, algebra, and English used the school building itself as the focus of a problem-solving project for 11th and 12th grade students. The school had been designed during the early '70s as an "open space"; interior walls had been added later. As a result, some classrooms were numbingly cold while others were too hot.

Teachers asked students to examine the school's heating and ventilating system to discover the cause of the problems, then research and propose a solution. After students had presented their solutions to their classmates, the class chose the best one—which was then proposed to the principal and school board. "Obviously, the kids had a lot of buy-in," Grady says.

■ At a rural school in Colorado, teachers asked students to advise the town government as to which of two local industries—ranching or mining— should be encouraged, based on the effects each had on the environment and the economy. One group of students who promoted ranching produced a video-tape making the case for raising buffalo instead of cattle.

■ At a Texas school in a town having trouble with its drinking water quality, teachers asked students to investigate the cause of the problem and to suggest ways to solve it without hurting the local economy.

Grady emphasizes that teachers need administrative support if efforts such as these are to succeed. "Administrators don't understand that it takes a lot more planning time" to create interdisciplinary curriculum, she says. Too often, such lessons get designed "between two and four a.m."

Scheduling is also critical to the success of efforts to fuse subject areas, says education consultant Heidi Hayes Jacobs, editor of ASCD's *Interdisciplinary Curriculum: Design and Implementation*. Schools must find ways to schedule opportunities for teachers to work together, and to provide longer blocks of time for students to pursue interdisciplinary projects, she believes. The flexibility or rigidity of the schedule can be the determining factor, Jacobs says: "Schedule is destiny."

Efforts to integrate subject areas are more likely to succeed if teachers learn about group process and develop the skills, such as negotiation, that will help them collaborate, says Pat Wasley, a senior researcher with the Coalition of Essential Schools at Brown University. Particularly at the high school level, teachers can influence others positively and "sail along," or they can alienate others and draw battle zones, Wasley says. Curriculum integration disrupts the department structure of the high school, she notes, and "that's a big deal."

Teachers need to be sensitive to interpersonal issues, Grady agrees. Interdisciplinary teaching may require them to serve on a team with someone they don't know—or don't respect, she points out. And interdisciplinary teams *must* have a leader to provide direction.

Krogh offers a caveat based on her own experience. Teachers who have created integrated units need to realize that this year's children might have different interests from last year's, she says. Krogh herself taught a class of four- and five-year-olds who constantly asked her, "When are we gonna do dinosaurs?" To capitalize on their interest, Krogh spent hours developing lesson plans on brontosaurs and stegosaurs. The children loved the unit, she says.

The next year, however, her students were apathetic to dinosaurs; the subject left them cold. "I was extremely frustrated," Krogh says. "I had all these wonderful materials." Yet, the following year, the class was again very responsive to the topic.

Krogh believes teachers need to honor students' own interests. "Listen to the children: they'll tell you," she advises. And she recommends that teachers not create units that last the entire year.

Start Small

When teachers decide to blend disciplines, they should "start with something fairly small and manageable," such as a short thematic unit, says

Kathleen Roth, an associate professor of teacher education at Michigan State University. "A [whole] curriculum organized around themes can be overwhelming to a teacher," she says.

Roth emphasizes the need for teachers to be reflective about the changes they make. Too often, she has seen teachers "buying into" the idea of interdisciplinary education without asking when and why it makes sense. When creating new lessons, teachers should ask themselves, "Would students be interested in this?" and, more important, "What would they be learning from this?" Developing curriculum that promotes critical thinking and deep understanding is not something many teachers have learned to do, Roth says.

In merging disciplines, teachers should avoid a level of intensity they can't sustain, says Robin Fogarty of IRI/Skylight Publishing, author of *The Mindful School: How to Integrate the Curricula*. Trying always to work in a team of five or more teachers, she cautions, will demand too much time and energy; it will also be difficult to schedule meetings everyone can attend. Therefore, teachers should consider doing "an intense model" only once a semester or so.

"Moving to more integrated, holistic learning won't happen overnight," Fogarty says. Instead, teachers should try "easing into it." A good way to start, she suggests, is to inventory what's already being done at the school—writing across the curriculum, for example—and build on those efforts.

Teachers should avoid making integrated activities too elaborate, agrees Bena Kallick, an education consultant from Westport, Conn. "Be careful not to make a three-ring circus out of it," she says, because if the effort is exhausting, teachers may never do it twice. Kallick also cautions teachers against "force fitting" their instruction around a theme, which she says can lead to superficial teaching.

Public support is another necessary ingredient to the success of interdisciplinary teaching.

"I don't believe the public has embraced inter-disciplinary education as something they think is important," says David Ackerman, superintendent of the Catalina Foothills School District in Tucson, Ariz. But that doesn't necessarily mean they're opposed to it, he adds.

One way to garner public support, Ackerman says, is to demonstrate that academic rigor is not being sacrificed on the altar of curriculum integration. The Humanities course at his district's high school, which combines history and English, has clearly defined performance expectations in both subjects, he says.

Allowing students to choose whether they take interdisciplinary classes can also help win community acceptance, Ackerman says, because "reform goes down better when people have choices." Efforts to combine disciplines in his district have succeeded, in part, because "students and families can select a pattern of courses that best matches their needs." Ackerman himself believes that a *portion* of each student's school experience should be interdisciplinary. "To never have a course that tries to break down discipline boundaries is to miss a valuable experience," he says.

Experts are cautiously optimistic that interdisciplinary teaching will become more popular in the future.

Enough teachers are dissatisfied with the status quo in schools, Grady believes, that they are willing to be risk takers; and these teachers are likely to be attracted to interdisciplinary education. "We need to start teaching students how to think, in much broader ranges than before"—including across disciplines, Grady says. "This is the way we need to go."

Kallick believes the degree to which interdisciplinary education will take hold depends on "how willing people are to really restructure." Will schools really let teachers work in teams, give them more planning time, and find new ways of assessing the quality of student work?

Kallick admits to being somewhat fearful about the recent popularity of teaching across disciplines. If interdisciplinary education becomes faddish and is practiced in superficial ways, it could lose credibility with teachers and the public. But "it will never go away," Kallick says. "It just plain makes sense. We live in an integrated world." ■

© Association for Supervision and Curriculum Development

Teaching Across Disciplines
Interest Remains High Despite Concerns over Coverage

By Scott Willis

In K–12 education, a field considered susceptible to fads, interdisciplinary teaching is notable for having held the interest of educators over time. After years of discussion and exploration, teachers remain attracted to the idea of integrating subject areas, for at least part of the school day, experts say. And many believe this interest is growing.

Interest in interdisciplinary teaching is "a wave that is gaining momentum in the United States, Canada, and Australia," says Robin Fogarty of IRI/Skylight Publishing, author of *The Mindful School: How to Integrate the Curricula.* "It's definitely a trend, not a fad."

When done well, interdisciplinary units enhance and enrich what students learn, experts say. For example, if students learn about the Revolutionary War while they also read a novel set during that period, they will learn more history *and* gain a better understanding of the novel.

Curriculum integration has taken root most firmly in the early grades, says Joan Grady, a senior program associate at the Mid-continent Regional Educational Laboratory (McREL) in Aurora, Colo. "Many elementary teachers, in their self-contained classrooms, perforce do a certain amount of interdisciplinary teaching," Grady says. Teachers at middle schools—where team teaching and block scheduling are common—do "a fair amount" of it. At the secondary level, teachers are doing less across disciplines, but "there's interest out there," Grady asserts.

Over the past few years, the focus of debate has changed, says education consultant Heidi Hayes Jacobs, author of ASCD's *Interdisciplinary Curriculum: Design and Implementation.* Today, there is no longer as much discussion among educators about *whether* to blend the disciplines, as about when, to what degree, and how best to do it, Jacobs says.

What accounts for the continuing appeal of interdisciplinary education? The widespread interest is fueled by a number of forces, Fogarty believes, including brain research on contextual learning; state and provincial mandates that promote interdisciplinary efforts; the middle school movement with its emphasis on team teaching; and the whole language movement at the elementary level, which cuts across disciplines.

"Teachers are desperately looking for ways to engage kids," says Pat Wasley, a senior researcher with the Coalition of Essential Schools at Brown University, and author of *Stirring the Chalk Dust: Tales of Teachers Changing Classroom Practice.* By breaking through discipline boundaries, teachers can make the curriculum more relevant and contemporary, she says, because they can embed knowledge and skills in real-life contexts, rather than teaching them from a dry textbook. Concepts from biology and social studies, for example, could be taught through a focus on bioengineering—a topical focus that students would find interesting. This approach also helps students understand the real-world *need* for what they learn, which makes them willing to work harder.

Concerns About Content

Despite its popularity, interdisciplinary teaching raises concerns among some parents and educators. The concern voiced most often is that moving from a discipline-based to a theme-based approach will cause important content to fall by the wayside. Especially at the upper grade levels, teachers fear that the "purity" of their disciplines will be lost in integrated units, Fogarty says. Teachers worry they won't be able to go into depth in their subject areas because they're trying to meet a thematic focus.

Another common concern is that, in integrated units, one discipline will be allowed to overshadow another. Liz Orme, who teaches at Montgomery Junior/Secondary School in Coquitlam, British Columbia, notes that the chronological framework of the social studies curriculum can "smother" the English curriculum, which is less concrete and sequential.

Teachers also worry that one subject will be used as a "handmaiden" to another. Math might become merely a tool of science, for example—no longer studied for its own sake. "English is used a lot as a tool," says Grady of McREL, who trains teachers in a process for developing "chunks" of integrated curriculum. In planning these "chunks," teachers often ask students to make presentations or write papers, but they neglect to include novels and poetry, she says.

Some educators say they have learned from experience that these fears are well-founded. Kathleen Roth, an associate professor of teacher education at Michigan State University who also teaches 5th grade science, was dissatisfied with the results of a year-long unit in which she took part. The unit, which blended social studies and science, was organized around a "1492" theme. Roth felt that the unit did not do enough to help students grow as scientific thinkers. "Despite careful, collaborative planning, I was unable to create activities that fit the theme and connected with the social studies activities while simultaneously engaging students in active, meaningful scientific inquiry," Roth has written. "We called this unit integrated science/social studies, but it really felt like social studies."

Her experience was not unusual, Roth believes. Thematic units often fail to focus on powerful ideas or organizing concepts from the disciplines, she says. In selecting concepts for such units, teachers often choose what fits best with the theme, rather than emphasizing the ideas that are most important and useful within the discipline. As a result, content is "compromised or diluted." Teachers shouldn't just assume that curriculum integration is inherently a good thing, Roth says. They should explore what *kinds* of integration yield benefits for student learning.

Experience with interdisciplinary teaching led Suzanne Krogh of Western Washington University to a similar conclusion. When developing her book, *The Integrated Early Childhood Curriculum*, Krogh took a sabbatical to teach 2nd grade, so she could "try everything out" in the classroom. She was badly shaken when a visitor asked her class what they were learning in social studies, and the children just looked at her blankly. "They didn't know what 'social studies' meant," Krogh realized. In trying hard to integrate content, she had failed to give her students any conception of the subject areas and their meaning—something she believes students should know and understand.

Since that time, Krogh has tempered her thinking about interdisciplinary efforts in general. She had assumed that the second edition of her book would take a more radical, far-reaching approach to integrating content than the first, she says. But in surveying the literature, she discovered a lot of concern (even among advocates of curriculum integration) that the integrity of specific subjects could be lost. Because she shared this concern, even at the early childhood level, she decided to retain the first edition's conservatism.

The concern over losing important content is "very reasonable," says Jacobs, who emphasizes that teachers should fuse the disciplines only when doing so allows them to teach important content more effectively. By providing a context for the knowledge and skills students learn, interdisciplinary teaching can improve students' retention, Jacobs notes. But if teachers feel that a particular effort to integrate content is "sabotaging" their work, they simply shouldn't do it.

Teachers might want to reflect on why they

feel that way, however. Often, when teachers begin to blend the disciplines, they feel "a nagging fear that they're not doing their job," says Wasley. Trained as single-discipline teachers, they worry that they may be "shirking their curriculum responsibilities."

This fear stems from the old conception of learning as simply the acquisition of content knowledge, Wasley says. If a teacher believes that students should learn a great deal of vocabularly in Biology I, for example, then using an interdisciplinary approach focused on broad concepts might constitute "shirking." But for many teachers today, Wasley notes, the goal is to ensure that students *understand* what they know. A teacher who wants students to understand interdependence within biological systems, for example, might better achieve that goal by using an integrated approach that pays less attention to vocabulary.

In a well-designed integrated unit, less is more, says Jane McGeehan, a former teacher who now works for the consulting firm Susan Kovalik and Associates in Kent, Wash. Although some topics will not be addressed, the most powerful skills and concepts from the disciplines can be woven into a yearlong theme that is relevant to young people's lives, she says. This approach gives students opportunities to *apply* knowledge—instead of just "going through the motions" of memorizing and then forgetting information.

Teachers can't be sure students really understand what they've learned unless students apply it in a different context, Jacobs believes. For example, a math teacher could find out what students *truly* know about statistics, she says, by asking them to apply statistics to demographic patterns in immigration.

Avoiding the Pitfalls

In revising the curriculum to focus on themes or problems, how can teachers prevent essential learnings from winding up on the cutting room floor?

Team planning is "vital" to ensure subject integrity, says Orme. When two or more subject-area experts plan curriculum together, "each person is going to protect her discipline," she says. When Orme, an English teacher, planned and taught a two-hour Humanities course with a social studies teacher, she was able to teach the same number of novels and poems as she had in English, but "what we got across was richer," because the literature was placed in a historical context. Now, as a teacher solely responsible for teaching Humanities, she gives "a real English slant" to social studies, she concedes, because English is her area of expertise.

The benefits gained when teachers represent—and defend—their disciplines during planning have been demonstrated in the Bellingham, Wash., schools. According to Peggy Taylor of the district's central office, a committee of Bellingham educators worked three months to develop an interdisciplinary curriculum framework, which is now being used in 75 classrooms.

Initially, the framework focused on math, science, social studies, and reading, Taylor says. It took only "a brief swipe" at music and physical education, listing songs and activities such as square dancing. This "cursory endorsement" did not satisfy some music and physical education teachers, who wanted to see "depth, and a spiral of skills" in their disciplines. At their own request, specialists in music and physical education, and a media technician, have been added to the interdisciplinary committee.

Teachers' defending their disciplines can be a two-edged sword, however, says Grady. Although teachers should protect the content that is integral to their subject areas, they shouldn't try to make their own disciplines dominant. Teachers also need to appreciate that sometimes another subject might take the lead, Grady says. "Next time it might be yours."

Another way to avoid losing important

content in interdisciplinary units is by paying explicit attention to standards and outcomes, experts say.

Because teachers in Bellingham were concerned about coverage of important content in interdisciplinary units, Taylor says, the district has emphasized the need for unit outcomes that are well articulated from the beginning. The "driving force" in planning, she says, is to ensure that "critical content" is clearly identified. Otherwise, "you can have cutesy activities, but what do they add up to?"

The process for curriculum planning that McREL promotes pays close attention to standards and benchmarks, says Grady. Typically, teachers select a theme or topic focus, then identify the standards—from their district or state, or from national subject-area groups—that must be embedded in instruction.

Teachers feel comfortable with the McREL approach because it yields curriculum strongly founded in standards, Grady says. Teachers *don't* feel "my subject is losing out," she says. And the standards basis makes the new curriculum easier to sell to parents, because educators can show that it's "not just a lot of fun activities that kids like to do."

Like discipline-based courses, interdisciplinary courses benefit from clearly defined performance expectations, says David Ackerman, superintendent of the Catalina Foothills School District in Tucson, Ariz. Teachers should be able to state, "By taking this course, students will be able to . . ." The performance expectations should make clear the "value-added dimension" of the interdisciplinary approach, Ackerman says, which should "help make the case for it."

Doing interdisciplinary teaching well is very powerful—but very difficult, Roth says. Although she was not happy with the "1492" unit, she had better success with another effort to merge science and social studies. In science, she taught her students about things that dissolve; in social studies, she taught about farming in the United States. Then she pulled the two subjects together by teaching about farmers' use of pesticides and insecticides, including what dissolves in rain water. Because interdisciplinary connections were made *after* students had a base of understanding in both subjects, they were "easier for the kids to grasp," she believes.

In planning integrated curriculum, teachers need to ask, "Is it a natural connection, or a forced and superficial one?" Roth says. "Naturally occurring links are extremely powerful." ∎

Choosing a Theme

By Scott Willis

Choosing a fruitful theme is critical to the success of an interdisciplinary unit, experts emphasize.

The theme or question chosen has to be broad enough that students can find an area of personal interest, says Pat Wasley of the Coalition of Essential Schools. "What is the relation between the elements in the garden?" will be a more productive question than something narrow, such as "What is soil?" A theme that is too broad, however, can be "a disaster," says Rick Lear, also of the Coalition, because, if everything fits into it, the theme becomes meaningless.

Education consultant Susan Kovalik suggests several criteria for choosing a good theme, in the form of questions teachers should ask themselves:
■ What is so important about this theme that it will promote future learning?
■ Does it have substance and application to the real world? ("Dinosaurs are dead," she notes, alluding to a popular theme.)
■ Are relevant materials readily available?
■ Is it meaningful and age-appropriate?
■ Does it tie into other units, enabling students to make generalizations and have greater understanding? (Themes must relate to one another, she says. It is a mistake to think "You do fish for one month, then simple machines for one month." Themes should "flow" logically.)
■ Is it worth the time needed to create and implement it?

Teachers need to guard against choosing themes that will "play well" with students but not yield much learning, warns David Perkins of Harvard's Project Zero. "Sometimes [units] are organized around trivial themes with no depth," he says. As an example, he cites the theme of "transportation," an arbitrary category that "doesn't boil down to much" as a means of integrating subject areas. "Evidence" is a better theme, he says, for several reasons:
■ It applies broadly to a wide range of subject areas. The question, "How do we know what we know?" applies to all subjects.
■ It discloses fundamental patterns. Discussion of "evidence" would lead to analytical concepts such as hypothesis, experiment, and deductive and inductive reasoning.
■ It reveals contrasts and similarities. For example, evidence in math consists of logical reasoning; in science, experimentation; in literature, textual analysis and interpretation. Hypothesis and conjecture, however, operate in all subject areas.

Another important criterion of a good theme, Perkins adds, is that it fascinates students once they get immersed in it.

Students' reactions to themes can be difficult to predict, however. Six teachers at the Fryeburg Academy in Fryeburg, Maine, collaborated to develop units on evolution, power, discovery, and revolutions, says Jan Hastings, a music teacher at the school. When they taught the first unit, on evolution, the teachers were pleased. But "the kids hated it. They said, 'We don't want to hear about the same thing in every class.'" Hastings attributes students' resentment to the fact that they had never been asked to think about the same concept in every subject area before.

Suzanne Krogh of Western Washington University had an entire class reject her dinosaur unit. She canceled it, despite the time and energy she had invested in preparing it. "The teacher has to be flexible and listen to what children are interested in," she says. Themes that capture young students' interest include marine ecology, the planetary system, and space exploration, she has found.

To avoid student apathy or rebellion, interdisciplinary themes should arise from students' own questions and concerns, says James Beane of the

National College of Education in Evanston, Ill. Themes and related activities should be "planned from scratch with kids," he believes, by surveying students or brainstorming with them. Such an approach taps students' interests and empowers them as learners.

Those who believe adolescents' interests are trivial or self-centered are simply mistaken, Beane says. Students have "tremendous concerns about the larger world," including such issues as world peace, the economy, racism, and protecting the environment. "They're very concerned about the future." *"We're not just saying to kids, 'What do you want to do?'" Beane emphasizes. Instead, the approach is tightly structured. Whatever themes are chosen should have "major self and social significance," he says.*

Instruction has more power if teachers build the curriculum around what students see as relevant right now, agrees Gordon Vars of Kent State University. Vars sees no reason to be concerned if students cite trivial interests. In the hands of a good teacher, he says, even something frivolous can lead to serious study. If the starting point is Nintendo, for example, students' explorations can encompass science, math, social studies, psychology, English, and technology.

Krogh confirms that students don't necessarily want to study pop-culture fluff. Intrigued by differences between languages, her class of 2nd graders at an international school in Spain asked to study language roots. The students created charts of languages that evolved from Latin, studied linguistics and geography, and traced the influence of the ancient Romans.

Such enthusiasm comes as no surprise to Wasley. When teachers honor students' natural investigative qualities, students produce sophisticated works, she says. "People like to create their own learning tasks." ■

© Association for Supervision and Curriculum Development

INDEX

ABOUT THE AUTHOR

Susan M. Drake is currently a professor in the graduate department of Brock University, St. Catharines, Ontario. She has a doctorate in curriculum from University of Toronto, and has taught at all levels of education—elementary, high school, adult education, and higher education. She has authored or co-authored six books, several of which are about integrated curriculum. Her latest book is *Creating Integrated Curriculum: Proven Ways to Increase Student Learning,* published by Corwin Press in 1998. This book offers a variety of models of integrated curriculum and teacher-developed applications of these models. She has also authored *Planning Integrated Curriculum: The Call to Adventure,* which outlined the myriad processes of integrating curriculum and the challenges associated with its implementation. She also authored a research paper for the Ministry of Ontario Education and Training in 1997 and provided background on interdisciplinary studies for high school reform policy. She has authored numerous articles on both the process and product of integration, and has been involved in extensive inservicing for teachers in the United States, Canada, South Africa, Thailand, and Japan.

ABOUT ASCD

Founded in 1943, the Association for Supervision and Curriculum Development is a nonpartisan, nonprofit education association, with international headquarters in Alexandria, Va. ASCD's mission statement: ASCD, *a diverse, international community of educators, forging covenants in teaching and learning for the success of all learners.*

Membership in ASCD includes a subscription to the award-winning journal *Educational Leadership*; two newsletters, *Education Update* and *Curriculum Update*; and other products and services. ASCD sponsors affiliate organizations in many states and international locations; participates in collaborations and networks; holds conferences, institutes, and training programs; produces publications in a variety of media; sponsors recognition and awards programs; and provides research information on education issues.

ASCD provides many services to educators—prekindergarten through grade 12—and to others in the education community, including parents, school board members, administrators, and university professors and students. For further information, contact ASCD via telephone: 800-933-2723 or 703-578-9600; fax: 703-575-5400; or e-mail: member@ascd.org. Or write to ASCD, 1703 N. Beauregard St., Alexandria, VA 22311-1714 USA. You can find ASCD on the World Wide Web at http://www.ascd.org.

ASCD's Executive Director is Gene R. Carter.

2000-01 EXECUTIVE COUNCIL

President: LeRoy Hay, Assistant Superintendent for Instruction, Wallingford Public Schools, Wallingford, Connecticut

President-Elect: Kay A. Musgrove, Associate Superintendent for Teaching and Learning, Franklin Special School District, Franklin, Tennessee

Immediate Past President: Joanna Choi Kalbus, Lecturer in Education, University of California at Riverside, Redlands, California

Martha Bruckner, Chair and Associate Professor, Department of Educational Administration and Supervision, University of Nebraska at Omaha, Omaha, Nebraska

David Chen, Dean, School of Education, Tel Aviv University, Israel

Richard L. Hanzelka, Director of General Education, Mississippi Bend Area Education Agency #9, Bettendorf, Iowa

Douglas E. Harris, Executive Director, Vermont Institute for Science, Math, & Technology, Vermont College, Montpelier, Vermont

Mildred Huey, Director of Curriculum/Federal Programs, York School District One, York, South Carolina

Sharon Lease, Deputy State Superintendent for Public Instruction, Oklahoma State Department of Education, Oklahoma City, Oklahoma

Leon Levesque, Superintendent, Lewiston School District, Lewiston, Maine

Francine Mayfield, Director, Elementary School-Based Special Education Programs, Seigle Diagnostic Center, Las Vegas, Nevada

Andrew W. Tolbert, Assistant Superintendent, Pine Bluff School District, Pine Bluff, Arkansas

Sandra K. Wegner, Associate Dean, College of Education, Southwest Missouri State University, Springfield, Missouri

Peyton Williams Jr., Deputy State Superintendent, Georgia State Department of Education, Atlanta, Georgia

Jill Dorler Wilson, Elementary School Principal, Pasadena Lakes Elementary, Pembroke Pines, Florida

Donald B. Young, Professor, Curriculum Research and Development Group, University of Hawaii, Honolulu, Hawaii